Author of more than fifty books, Michael Moorcock is one of Britain's most popular and prolific writers. Known to millions for the remarkable 'Elric' stories, his many awards include the Nebula Award (*Behold the Man*), the World Fantasy Award (*The Warhound and the World's Pain*) and the Guardian Fiction Award (*The Condition of the Muzak*). His recent novels include *The Laughter of Carthage* and *The City in the Autumn Stars*.

MICHAEL MOORCOCK

Wizardry and Wild Romance

A study of epic fantasy

VGSF

VGSF is an imprint of Victor Gollancz Ltd
14 Henrietta Street, London WC2E 8QJ

First published in Great Britain 1987
by Victor Gollancz Ltd

First VGSF edition 1988

Copyright © 1987 Michael Moorcock

British Library Cataloguing in Publication Data
Moorcock, Michael, *1939-*
　　Wizardry and wild romance:　　A study of
epic fantasy.
　　1. Fiction in English, to 1987. Fantasy –
Critical studies
　　I. Title
823'.00915

ISBN 0-575-04324-5

Printed and bound in Great Britain
by Cox & Wyman Ltd, Reading

For Jim Cawthorn

who introduced me to so many good
writers and whose illustrations over
the past thirty years have given me
so much pleasure and inspiration...

And for Brian Tawn and Pete Knifton
and other discriminating readers of
fantastic fiction for whom this book
will provide a few revelations and a
fair amount for them to disagree with.
And to the memory of
Bill Butler, who died in
his sleep, aged 43, 20th
October, 1977.

Wizardry
and
Wild Romance

Contents

And you love take my right hand,
Come join the faery folks' last dance;
Then we'll sleep and dream of Elfland,
Her wizardry and wild romance.

Wheldrake,
The Elvish Rune,
1877

Introduction

Hobbes, in order to daunt the reader from objecting to his friend Davenant's want of invention, says of these fabulous creations in general, in his letter prefixed to the poems of Gondibert, that "impenetrable armours, enchanted castles, invulnerable bodies, iron men, flying horses, and a thousand other such things, are easily feigned by them that dare". These are girds at Spenser and Ariosto. But, with leave of Hobbes (who translated Homer as if on purpose to show what execrable verses could be written by a philosopher), enchanted castles and flying horses are not easily feigned, as Ariosto and Spenser feigned them; and that just makes all the difference.

Leigh Hunt, *Imagination and Fancy*, 1844

I have no intention in this book of "defining" the term epic fantasy. Neither do I expect my polemics to convince anyone already opposed to my points of view. In general I intend to discuss the subject of Romantic Fantasy (with the obvious exception of its modern commercial corruption describing a sentimental love story) and specifically touch on that area of fabulous romance whose writers invent their own Earthly histories and geographies. Romantic fiction (especially that by South American writers) is enjoying something of a vogue and is currently accepted as a respectably serious mode by our literary establishments. Actually most European fiction originally contained strong romantic elements and it only gradually became fashionable to exclude them by the mid-19th century when the rift between popular and "serious" fiction began to manifest itself. It could be said that Jane Austen established our taste for the novel of manners but it was Victorian middle-class morality which established that type of fiction as the only respectable form (F. R. Leavis went one step further, insisting that only this kind of fiction could reasonably be called art). Nonetheless, all the great 19th-century realists introduced strong strands of romance into their work and some of them, notably Flaubert with *Salammbô* and Meredith with *The Shaving of Shagpat*, produced gorgeous works of full-blooded and fantastic invention.

Since that time it seems that almost every realist has had at least one romance in them, from Henry James (*The Turn of the Screw*) to Angus Wilson (*The Old Men at the Zoo*). In recent years the gradual acceptance of romantic methods by critics and academics has allowed novelists previously accepted as realists to indulge themselves with fantasies, parables, symbols, allegories and whatnot, often with disastrous effects. I have the idea of a new school emerging, of *would-be* Romantics, desperately striving to discover fresh sensibilities in the way repressed products of the middle classes tried to loosen up with drugs and sentimental egalitarianism in the sixties. These people learned the school rules too well, however, and the main impression I have of their fabulations is of red elbows and other miscellaneous bits of anatomy poking out through holes they have, with much effort and personal discomfort, rubbed in the straitjacket.

I must admit that my own taste is primarily for the likes of George Eliot, Meredith and Conrad, but I still enjoy and respect a good romance if it has wit as well as epic elements and if the characters are not too "distanced". I've no admiration at all for the rafts of Robert E. Howard and J. R. R. Tolkien imitations presently feeding commercial genre demands and will not deal with them here in any detail. I'm chronically unable to enjoy most formula fiction, be it by Larry Niven, Norman Mailer or Margaret Drabble.

Epic fantasy can be seen as a late development of that element of the Romantic Revival that began in 1762 with the publication of Macpherson's "Ossian" cycle, was continued through Walpole's *Castle of Otranto* (1764) and Percy's *Reliques of Ancient English Poetry* (1765), Chatterton's *Rowley Poems* (1777), the *Lyrical Ballads* (1798) of Coleridge and Wordsworth, Scott's *Lay of the Last Minstrel* (1805), Tennyson's *Poems* (1842), given further impetus by Carlyle's translations and studies of the German Romanticists (such as Burger, Tieck, Hoffman, Musäus, but also Goethe and Schiller) and his books like *Past and Present* (1843) which was to have such an evident influence on Morris, through Rossetti (*The Germ*, 1850), Ruskin (*The Stones of Venice*, 1851-3), to Morris himself (*The Defence of Guenevere*, 1858).

The earlier origins of epic fantasy, of course, are in a direct line from the fabulous epics of Gilgamesh, Ulysses, Finn Mac Coul, Siegfried, Arthur, Charlemagne and, again primarily through Morris, the Icelandic sagas.

If I fail to define epic fantasy (except very roughly and in passing) in this essay I shall also fail to defend it for its own sake. As with anything else, only a little is outstandingly good and much of it, while it has attractive qualities of enthusiasm and vitality, has no literary merit. I'm unable to muster much nostalgic response to old pulp magazines, comic books or that school of fiction exemplified by Oxford's deceased *Inklings*. I admire intelligent, disciplined, imaginative entertainment which provides me with some perspective on my own life. This essay, therefore, cannot for me be the celebration of a form. It can only praise individuals.

Similarly I will not be mentioning my own work. I shall, as it is, only be able to deal briefly with many of the writers discussed, so if I fail to support my cases as fully as I should, I apologize. Most of the sweeping statements found here may be seen as the opening stages of a debate rather than final pronouncements of my own faith!

H. P. Lovecraft, that somewhat inadequate describer of the indescribable, says in his book *Marginalia*:

> Modern Science has, in the end, proved an enemy to art and pleasure; for by revealing to us the whole sordid and prosaic basis of our thoughts, motives and acts, it has stripped the world of glamour, wonder, and all those illusions of heroism, nobility, and sacrifice which used to sound so impressive when romantically treated. Indeed, it is not too much to say that psychological discovery, and chemical, physical and psychological research have largely destroyed the element of emotion among informed and sophisticated

17

people by resolving it into its component parts.

There is pathos in this statement, as well as a rather unappealing kind of aggression which we still find expressed by the likes of Barbara Cartland, Mary Whitehouse, Malcolm Muggeridge and Colin Wilson, and for me it also explains why I can never enjoy a Lovecraft story. His words are all but meaningless. The heroism, nobility and sacrifice of Rudolf Hess may be moving, but they are only "impressive" if we understand the psychology involved. I believe that critical dissection of the fantasy story into its components does not detract from the story. Rather it adds a new dimension to it; a dimension which to me is far more interesting and rewarding. In an article published in the *Woman Journalist* (Spring 1963), J. G. Ballard wrote:

I feel that the writer of fantasy has a marked tendency to select images and ideas which directly reflect the internal landscapes of his mind, and the reader of fantasy must interpret them on this level, distinguishing between the manifest content, which may seem obscure, meaningless or nightmarish, and the latent content, the private vocabulary of symbols drawn by the narrative from the writer's

mind. The dream worlds, synthetic landscapes and plasticity of visual forms invented
by the writer of fantasy are external equivalents of the inner world of the psyche. . . .

Einstein, Freud and Jung between them have
broadened rather than destroyed the scope of the
artist and broadened the range of enjoyment which
the intelligent reader can derive from fiction. In a
romance the "real" world of the social novel is
reversed; the protagonists are placed in landscapes
directly reflecting the inner landscapes of their
minds. A hero might range the terrain of his own
psyche, encountering, as other characters, various
aspects of himself. A good fantasy story should be
able to lead us to greater self-understanding.

Therefore the main fascination of the fantasy
story could lie in its manipulation of direct sub-
conscious symbols. The mingled attraction and
revulsion often felt by its readers might well
express the combined curiosity and fear of seeing
too deeply into themselves. If our "irrational"
dreams are potent images "explained" by the
semi-conscious mind and blended into some sort
of rough plot, so fantasy stories take the same
material and attempt the same sort of job, with the
object of convincing our rational minds, even if
only temporarily. Too much rationalization, and
we get a certain kind of rather dull science fiction;

just enough to organize the images and give symbolic shape to and perhaps understanding of our strongest, most secret impulses, and we get a good fantasy story. Add superior language or painting, and we get a Coleridge or an Ernst.

Epic fantasy can offer a world of metaphor in which to explore the rich, hidden territories deep within us. And this, of course, is why epic romances, romantic poetry, grotesques, fascinated painters and illustrators for centuries, just as fabulous and mythological subjects have always inspired them, as representations of this inner world. The romance's prime concern is not with character or narrative but with the evocation of strong, powerful images; symbols conjuring up a multitude of sensations to be used (as mystics once used distorting mirrors, as romantics used opium or, latterly, LSD) as escape from the pressures of the objective world or as a means of achieving increased self-awareness.

In some cases the writer and the illustrator have been combined in one person (Blake, Rossetti, Wyndham Lewis, Peake). Even if we exclude all the children's writers (Ruskin/Doyle, Carroll/Tenniel, Nesbit/Millar, Baum/Neill) who have had long associations with particular illustrators, there are a good few adult writers of fantasy who have enjoyed similar relationships — Dunsany and Sime, Cabell and Papé, Burroughs and St John, Howard and Frazetta. There are innumerable versions of Goethe, Poe, the *Arabian Nights*, Hans Andersen, Hoffman, Wagner, from the "Golden Age" of illustration. More recently, artists have been attracted to the work of epic fantasts like Tolkien, Hodgson, Howard, Leiber as inspiration for elaborate posters, lavishly illustrated books and comic strip adaptations. Many of the best artists are attracted to these works because they tend to emphasize human aspiration and foibles, their pathos and ecstasy, more directly than, say, science fiction (itself, really, only a branch of fabulous romantic fiction). Since the 1960s there has been a huge revival of the art of book illustration, primarily based around this kind of fiction. From somewhat crude beginnings, where artists (as the bad ones still do) hid poor draughtsmanship behind elaborate grotesqueries, there is now developing a variety of excellent illustrators.

If, currently, the morbidly sexual aspects of fantasy are in danger of becoming a stale convention by virtue of repetition, if distorted perspective and two-dimensional sensationalism, inherited from the conventions of the commercial comic strip, still tend to dominate the magazines, comics and posters, there are some signs of artists maturing both technically and emotionally. We can hope that their work becomes increasingly subtle and humane; their ambitions growing as their mastery of their art grows and their talents — inspired by an increasing number of peers, by an increasing public appreciation of good work, by the appearance, in recent years, of publishers who both respect the artists and are prepared to pay them fair rates — blooming as luxuriantly throughout Europe and America as they did in the "Golden Age" of Willette, Beardsley, Klimt, Mucha, Dulac, Bull, Sime, Pogany, the Robinsons and all the other fabulous illustrators who emerged between the 1880s and the beginning of the first world war.

Lastly, it could be argued that the present time is about the worst in which to try to assess current developments in fantastic fiction. We are currently experiencing a boom in this, the most recent of publishing/bookselling categories. Whereas writers of epic fantasy might, like me, get irritated a few years ago because bookshops insisted on putting all their work in the sf section, now those same writers inhabit a section marked simply Fantasy and have covers on their books which are almost invariably indistinguishable from a hundred others. Therefore it's pretty hard to see the wood for the trees. I have read a fair number of recent books in this category but cannot claim to have read the best or the worst. Most of them are simply bad, several show promise, one or two are by writers of genuinely original talent. If names are omitted by me it is not of any special significance. I have no wish to attack the work of new and young writers, many of whom will doubtless find their feet in genre work before producing something more individual. In the main I have saved my polemics for writers who already have large (and often highly inflated) reputations. I have also preferred to quote those writers I admire, rather than take to task those I dislike. I hope that my relish for the work of the writers I enjoy will be what the reader remembers best from this essay.

I would like to thank various people for their help on this book. Firstly, as always, my wife Linda Steele, who read the text and helped produce the final edited version. Parts of this essay have appeared in different forms in *Science Fantasy* magazine, 1963–64 (commissioned by E. J. Carnell), in *Foundation* (editor Malcolm Edwards) and elsewhere, or have been given as talks to the Second World Fantasy Convention (who kindly invited me as Guest of Honour, New York, 1976), the Oxford Literary Society, the Cambridge Literary Society, Eton College Literary Society and others, to whom I am very grateful. "Epic Pooh" was published in pamphlet form by the British Fantasy Society, 1976. Parts have also appeared in the *London Daily News*, *Exploring Fantasy Worlds*, Borgo Press, 1985, and *Fantasists on Fantasy*, Avon Books, 1984. The original text was written at the request of Philip Dunn of the now defunct Pierrot Publishing. The revised text was commissioned by David Hartwell (then chief editor of Timescape Books). Thanks also to John Clute, for reading the manuscript and giving me his useful comments. A version of "Origins" was originally written in 1964 for Langdon Jones's magazine *Tensor*, but never published. I'm grateful to Mr Jones for supplying me with the only existing copy. People have been helpful in making suggestions for reading and so on. Among these are David Tate, Colin Greenland. Terri Windling, Brian Tawn, Roz Kaveney, Chelsea Quinn Yarbro, Lisa Tuttle and last but not least Messrs Dave Gibson and Ted Ball (of Fantasy Centre bookshop) and John Eggeling (of Phantasmagoria Books) who supplied many of the titles.

Michael Moorcock
Ingleton, W. Yorks,
August 1977 &
Fulham Road, London,
December 1985

I

Origins

Such a doze as I then enjoyed, I find compatible
with indulging the best and deepest cogitations
which at any time arise in my mind. I chew the
cud of sweet and bitter fancy, in a state betwixt
sleeping and waking, which I consider so highly
favourable to philosophy, that I have no doubt
some of its most distinguished systems have
been composed under its influence. My servant
is, therefore, instructed to tread as if upon down
— my door-hinges are carefully oiled — and all
appliances used to prevent me from being
prematurely and harshly called back to the
broad waking-day of a laborious world. My
custom, in this particular, is so well known, that
the very school-boys cross the alley on tip-toe,
betwixt the hours of four and five. My cell is the
very dwelling of Morpheus. There is indeed a
bawling knave of a broom-man, *quem ego* — but
this is matter for the Quarter-Sessions.

Sir Walter Scott, Introduction to *Peveril of
the Peak*

Perhaps the main fascination of epic fantasy is
that there have been few basic changes in it for

centuries. I am referring specifically to that body of prose fiction distinguished from myth, legend and folk-tale by its definite authorship and because it does not genuinely purport to be a true account of historical or religious events. Therefore the *Nibelungenlied, La Chanson de Roland, Le Morte d'Arthur* by Malory or *Le Cid* by Corneille are not fantasy fiction.

For the purposes of discussion the *Arabian Nights* or Moncrif's *Adventures de Zeloïde et d'Amanzarifdine* and many other groups of Oriental stories must also be set aside. The body of literature incorporating marvels and fantasies is so vast that it would be impossible in a short book to discuss it all.

Fantastic fiction, as opposed to the folk epic, is written for a particular audience at a particular time. Although it borrows images and cadences from poetry it is almost never poetic. It caters for current tastes; it takes the elements from the mother-body and presents them in popular and sensational form, working them into shapes and styles owing much to the demands of fashion. Though occasionally it will transcend these limitations it rarely outlives its contemporary audience. Popular fantasy fiction is not to be confused with the work of Spenser, Milton, Goethe, the major Romantics, *Ossian* and the Celtic Romance, satirists like Anatole France in, say, *La Révolte des anges*, allegorists such as Bunyan and Wyndham Lewis (or, during the later part of his career, John Cowper Powys), Hesse, Calvino or Borges. Epic fantasy includes *The Lord of the Rings*, *Conan the Conqueror* and *Palmerin of England*.

Palmerin de Ingelaterra (1547–48) and thousands like it were to the public of the 16th century what *Star Wars*, *Jaws*, *King Kong* and dinosaur and vampire movies are to the public of the 20th. They are called "decadent" or "artificial" romances and today most of them are, like most of the Gothic novels and oriental tales of the late 18th and early 19th centuries, virtually unreadable. *Palmerin* was, with *Amadis of Gaul*, one of the chivalric romances which escaped burning by the barber and the curate in *Don Quixote*, Cervantes' satire on such books. It was regarded, therefore, as a cut above the rest. Nonetheless these romances were fantasies in that their chief purpose was to amaze and shock. They are packed with wizards, magic weapons, cloaks of invisibility, beautiful sorceresses, flying machines and diving bells of various unlikely kinds, magic cups, rings, crowns, shoes, horses and castles; ogres, dwarves, monsters, malevolent spirits, helpful spirits, black curses, doom, tragedy — and a hero of incredible youth, good looks and prowess who is out to rescue a heroine of incredible youth, beauty and virtue.

Before heaven, your worship should read what I have read, concerning Felixmarte of Hyrcania, who with one backstroke cut asunder five giants through the middle, as if they had been so many bean-cods. . . . At another time he encountered a great and powerful army, consisting of about a million six hundred thousand soldiers, all armed from head to foot, and routed them as if they had been a flock of sheep. But what will you say of the good Don Cirongilo of Thrace? who was so stout and valiant . . . that once as he was sailing on a river, seeing a fiery serpent rise to the surface of the water, he immediately threw himself upon it, and getting astride its scaly shoulders squeezed its throat with both hands with so much force that the serpent, finding itself in danger of being choked, had no other remedy but to plunge to the bottom of the river, carrying with him the knight, who would not quit his hold; and when they reached the bottom, he found himself in such a fine palace and beautiful gardens, that it was wonderful; and presently the serpent turned into an old man, who said so many things to him that the like was never heard.

(*Don Quixote*)

Deriving from the Romances of Arthur,

Charlemagne and the Cid, owing something to Greek and Roman epics, something to fable and a little to history, borrowing language and manners from the metrical epics, from Ariosto, from *Aucassin et Nicolette*, the decadent Chivalric Romances had superficial resemblances to the originals but lacked their beauty of language and their genuine tragic elements. It is the mark of the commercial writer that they cheerfully disguise or dispense with the tragic implications of their material, sentimentalize relationships, intentions, even landscape, if it pleases their specific audience.

The Gothic Romance, which grew to popularity during the Romantic Revival, had much of its origins in the Chivalric Romance, but emphasized the element of terror and attempted, usually, to rationalize the supernatural element. It replaced chivalric notions with the ideals of its predominantly bourgeois audience. It made use of techniques developed by Defoe, Richardson or Fielding and no longer bore any resemblance to folk-literature.

However, in its use of archetypal characters, scenery and plots, the Gothic was still connected very closely to the Chivalric Romance, just as the modern tale of lost lands, prehistoric civilizations, fairy kingdoms or distant planets is connected to them both.

It is likely that a student of five hundred years

hence will see little difference between all of these. As the Gothic lost popularity and passed its lasting qualities into the general mainstream of fiction so, for instance, will the Science Fiction Romance leave its mark only on juvenile adventure stories and on the range of techniques available to the writer of non-category fiction.

Conscious art is on the whole lacking from the decadent Romance. Ornate and elaborate euphemism is substituted for the direct, simple language of the metrical romance or the poetry of *Orlando Furioso*. The sense of high tragedy found in the story of Tristram and Isoud is never apparent. In place of these are marvels upon marvels. The magical and supernatural elements in the great epics rarely dominated the human conflict. They served, symbolically, to heighten it. To modern readers of these epics the weighty narrative machinery, the dialogues and diversions, the archaisms are forgotten as the story gathers force, finding constant echoes in the readers' own experiences, resonances in their remembered dreams. Though concerned with deeds of daring, magic, human love there are no such resonances in the decadent Romance and so a modern reader's interest soon flags. To keep them reading, such a book must be written in more or less idiomatic language, in a certain kind of undemanding tone, for it is offering nothing but sensation and escapism.

Instead of:

> He gave him a good sword in his hand,
>   His head therewith for to keep;
> And there where the wall was lowest,
>   Anon down did they leap.
>
> By that the cock began to crow,
>   The day began to spring;
> The sheriff found the jailor dead,
>   The common bell made he ring.
>
> He made a cry throughout the town,
>   Whether he be yeoman or knave,
> That could bring him Robin Hood,
>   His warison he should have.
>   (*A Tale of Robin Hood*, c. 1350)

We get:

When he was seven years old, King Languines and his queen and household, passing through his kingdom from one town to another, came to the castle of Gandales, where they were feasted; but the Child of the Sea, and Gandalin, and the other children were removed to the back court, that they might not be seen. . . .

> (Southey's 1807 translation of *Amadis of Gaul*, Montalvo, 1508)

Then Palmerin and Trineus, snatching their

lances from their dwarves, and clasping their helmets, galloped amain after the giant, and Palmerin, having gotten a sight of him, came posting amain, saying: "Stay, traitorous thief, for thou mayst not so carry away her, that is worth the greatest lord in the world!" and with these words, gave him a blow on the shoulder, that he struck him besides his elephant. . . .

> (*Palmerin de Oliva*, c. 1511, quoted in
> Beaumont's *Knight of the Burning Pestle*,
> c. 1610)

Palmerin of England was very popular in Tudor England and has a sequel, *Palmerin de Oliva*. Allegedly written by a king of Portugal and sometimes thought to be the work of an unknown woman it was probably by Francisco de Moroes. *Amadis of Gaul* was also Portuguese in origin. This was the most imitated. The original four printed volumes were followed by about fifty sequels from almost as many imitators.

Amadis is included in the body of Romance usually termed Peninsular since it originated in Spain, Portugal and Italy. It is marked by a heavy Oriental influence and it was probably the same influence (stemming from such works as the *Arabian Nights*) which gave it its highly fantastic flavour.

These first four volumes of *Amadis* retain much of the drama of their earlier counterparts. This is primarily because they hinge on a classical plot and retain the range of archetypes. Because the average reader is not likely to have a copy to hand I intend to give here the only plot summary to be found in this book.

Amadis is born of an illegitimate union between Elisena, daughter of the King of Brittany, and King Perion of "Gaul" (probably Wales). Because of the stigma he is placed in a coracle and thrown into a river which runs to the sea. The coracle is found by Sir Gandales of Scotland who rears the boy with Gandalin, his son. He is nicknamed "the Child of the Sea", and he and Gandalin become inseparable. Sir Gandales knows that his foster child is the son of a king, since there is a note to that effect in the coracle, as well as an assortment of tokens to prove it.

"Passing through his kingdom from one town to another", King Languines of Scotland and his wife stay at the castle of Sir Gandales where they take a fancy to "the Child of the Sea" and his foster brother, bringing them to court as companions for their son Agraies. Little do any of them know that Languines's queen is actually Amadis's aunt. Soon we hear that Perion and Elisena have married. Amadis is legitimate! The couple have another son, Galaor, who is kidnapped by a giant, one

Gandalac, who plans to bring the boy up to avenge a wrong done him. A simple-minded soul, Gandalac gives Galaor into the keeping of a hermit who moulds him into a heroic and chivalrous youth. Perion and Elisena have a third son, Florestan, who serves no narrative purpose save to make the story more confusing. Giants and evil knights are fought by Amadis, Galaor and Florestan, with Gandalin tagging along as squire, but the brothers are still unaware of their relationship.

Then Perion decides to visit Languines's court at the same time as Lisuarte, King of Great Britain, who has brought Oriana, his daughter, with him. Oriana will become the story's heroine. After many, many pages of confused activity, Amadis accomplishes a quantity of doughty deeds and then his parentage is discovered. There is a full-scale reunion somewhat reminiscent of *The Man Who Was Thursday* or one of those skits on comic-strip super-heroes who reveal their secret identities all at once. The love of Amadis for Oriana is declared and we're off on a new set of adventures which are of a simpler construction and easier to follow. They are extraordinarily reminiscent of an Edgar Rice Burroughs yarn. The mistaken identity theme is familiar in all fiction and is often used to maintain certain conventional tensions in narratives which would otherwise fall to pieces after chapter three.

The set of stories is quite sharply divided between the initial tangle ending with recognitions
and joyful discovery, a long episode involving a
misunderstanding between the lovers (shades of
P. G. Wodehouse as well as Edgar Rice Burroughs)
and a kidnapping sequence where Oriana is taken
to the enchanted Firm Island and Amadis has to
rescue her. The fourth volume ends on this note.

Also in the latter two sequences we are introduced to Urganda the Unknown, a beneficent
sorceress, mysterious and wise, and Arcalaus, who
has been described as "an enchanter-at-arms" and
"one of the largest knights in the world who were
not giants". Amadis and Galaor are the two central
characters here and they are contrasted quite well
— Amadis remaining true to Oriana throughout,
whereas Galaor is always indulging in diversions
of love. The most concentrated fantastic element
is in the Firm Island sequence.

The Firm Island had been the home of Apollidon, "the sagest of enchanters", who had lived
there with his wife Grimanesa. He had built a
huge, jewel-studded castle and gardens and
orchards that bloomed and bore fruit throughout
the year. "Never had been such magnificence, nor
such marvels as the lord of this land gathered
together by his wealth and by his magic arts."
However, though he had hoped to spend his old age
on the Firm Island, Apollidon was asked to go to

Greece and there be crowned Emperor — "Then he left the Firm Island, with all its wonders, as a heritage to any knight who should prove as brave in arms as himself and as loyal in love to a lady not less fair and faithful than his own wife. To test the virtues of all aspirants, he laid mystic spells on the island, only to be broken by him who should be its lord. At the entrance to the gardens was an arch that could be safely passed by none but true lovers; and in the midst of them stood a Forbidden Chamber, fast closed to all but the knight and lady destined to achieve such great adventure. A hundred years had passed since the spell was laid, and a hundred knights had vainly sought to break it, when Amadis came with his kinsman to visit the Firm Island."

Amadis, Agraies, Galaor and Florestan come to the Arch of True Lovers which is guarded by a huge copper giant with a trumpet at its mouth. If an untrue lover tries to enter, the trumpet will blast him down with smoke and flames, but if he is true, music will issue from the trumpet. Agraies dashes through the gate and the trumpet blows sweet music and exquisite perfume.

"On the other side he came to statues of Apollidon and Grimanesa so artfully fashioned that he thought they smiled on him, and at their feet a table of jasper on which were carved the names of those knights who had come through aforetime.

Now, while he read he saw with amazement his own name springing to view. . . ."

Amadis also enters and sees his name appear, but his brothers demur — they are pretty sure they won't get sweet music and perfume. . . .

As Amadis and Agraies stroll about the beautiful gardens, Amadis's dwarf servant Ardian tells them that his brothers have got themselves into a mess. They have asked where the Forbidden Chamber lies and are debating whether to pass by the two pillars, one brass, one marble, which are on its path.

Florestan reaches the brazen pillar — "But ere he had reached it was soon to be fighting as if with the air. From all sides hailed upon him heavy blows dealt by invisible enemies, and when he struck back he felt his sword's edge turned upon ghostly weapons besetting him at every step." Florestan is hurled back at his brother's feet to lie as though dead. At this Galaor plunges in, makes out a little better, but is finally also hurled back. They are soon revived, however, as the cousins turn up. Agraies tries his luck and is unsuccessful. "None can fight through this enchantment but the peer of Apollidon who devised it," says the Governor of the Island. Amadis, of course, wins through to the Forbidden Chamber and the enchantment is broken.

This episode serves to prove to Oriana that

Amadis is a true lover after all. But the story isn't over. Further complications arise and Amadis disguises himself as Beltenbros, since he doesn't know that Oriana no longer hates him and has been living in a hermitage mourned as dead by his friends. As "Beltenbros" he comes home to find a war brewing between the King of Ireland (whose son he killed earlier) and King Lisuarte. Disguised in black and silver armour he joins the ranks of Lisuarte and there follows a battle scene between Cildadan of Ireland and Lisuarte of Great Britain which is reminiscent of the battles for which Robert E. Howard is famous. Here is a further quote from Moncrieff's excellent précis in the Gresham *Romance and Legend of Chivalry* (c. 1912):

Lisuarte welcomed Beltenbros, whose aid he could not refuse, since he now got news how was lost to him one of his trustiest warriors, Arban of Wales. He had been made prisoner by the wife of Famongomadan in revenge for her husband's death, and was pining in that giant's dungeons till the king were able to deliver him. Beltenbros made up the tale of his party, all of them famous knights of their time. There were the brothers of Amadis, and his cousin Agraies of Scotland; and Gandalac, Galaor's foster-father, with his sons Gavus and Palomir, Bramadil; and Nicoran, Keeper of the Perilous Bridge, with Dragonis and Palomar, and Pinorante; Gimontes, the king's nephew; the renowned Sir Bruneo of Bonamar, who, before Amadis, had achieved the passage of the True Lover's Arch, also his brother Branfil; and Sir Guilan the Pensive; and good old Sir Grumedan, who bore the king's banner in the centre of the troop, and Ladasin, and Galvanes, and Olivas; and many another whose name should not be forgotten.

On the adverse side, also, were chiefs of renown, and some of gigantic stature, such as Cartadaque, Albadanzor, and Gadancuriel, whom King Cildadan placed in the front of his ranks. He missed that day Famongomadan and his mighty son Basagente, laid low by Beltenbros on their way to take part in the battle. But not less fearful was the giant Mandanfabul, lord of the Isle of the Vermillion Tower, who with ten of his like were placed in the rear on a hill, with orders not to engage till they saw the enemy broken and weary, then to rush down upon King Lisuarte and kill him or carry him off prisoner.

The trumpet gave the signal for both lines to close, breaking upon each other like waves foaming with steel. The ground shook under the crash of that onset, in which many a man

went down, and many a horse galloped away
without a rider. Soon all the field was hidden
in clouds of dust, where the fighters, panting
for heat and rage, were mixed in a confused
struggle; and those who looked on with throb-
bing hearts could not tell how it went with
friend or foe. But like a thunderbolt gleamed
through the medley that silver knight on a
black horse, that kept ever close to the old
king, when, caring not to live unless victori-
ous, he threw himself into the hottest press.

The battle lasts half a day and all are weary —
then "through the thinned ranks swooped Mandanfabul with his band of fresh fighters, like kites
upon their prey, and came charging towards the
royal banner." They carry Lisuarte off, but Belten-
bros/Amadis sees Mandanfabul riding away with
the king and gives chase ... "he soon came up
with Mandanfabul, and fetched him such a mighty
blow as not only shore off the giant's right arm, but
beneath it cut through Lisuarte's armour and drew
his blood. Mandanfabul, losing control of his
horse, was carried away bleeding to death."
Amadis returns to rally the flagging knights.
"Then over all the clang and clamour rang out his
warcry:
  'Gaul! Gaul! I am Amadis!'"
And, given fresh courage by the sight of the

famed hero, the knights of Amadis beat the knights of the King of Ireland.

In this episode we are given a mystic prophecy from Urganda the Unknown; together with various monsters and giants and magics of all kinds. It is scarcely different in any way (save for the element of chivalry) from, say, Howard's *Conan the Conqueror*, whose only virtue is that its plot is slightly less rambling and it is considerably shorter.

As an example of one of the best artificial Romances, I think *Amadis* deserves its preservation. Its imitators, though containing many more marvels (a large number directly derived from Arabian tales), are interesting only for their variety of enchantments and spells. *Palmerin of England* is one of the few real rivals, though it is quite similar in most ways to *Amadis*.

The Chivalric Romance, together with old English metrical ballads (as published in Percy's *Reliques*) and Macpherson's *Ossian* forgeries, influenced two important and connected strains in English literature — the historical novel of Scott and others — and the Gothic "tale of terror" which in its earliest form at least usually had a mediaeval setting.

Many critics have discussed the reasons for their appeal. Robert Graves's *The White Goddess* provides a semi-mystical explanation; Jung's *Modern*

Man in Search of a Soul provides a psychological one. The best single work on purely literary aspects is probably Mario Praz's *The Romantic Agony*.

The first Gothic romance to call itself that and to begin the vogue for tales of terror was Walpole's *Castle of Otranto* (1764). Walpole's main interest was art and architecture. By "Gothic" he meant pre-Renaissance. Just as *Don Quixote* and *The Knight of the Burning Pestle* had appeared as a reaction against the Romance, Walpole's book was a reaction against the prevailing classicism of the Age of Reason, directly opposed in its intentions to the realistic fiction of Defoe, Richardson or Fielding. With Macpherson's *Fingal* (1762) and Percy's *Reliques of Ancient English Poetry* (1765) it is generally thought to be one of the chief landmarks of the beginning of the Romantic Revival. Clara Reeve's *The Champion of Virtue, a Gothic Story* (1777) was written in deliberate homage to Walpole. Set in the 15th century it contains a great deal of description of romantic landscape and architecture but only one supernatural element (a ghost). It was later reissued as *The Old English Baron* and, like Walpole's romance, is still in print.

Although neither book is, in itself, very readable, they are important because they represent a watershed in the development of fiction. They did not merely look back to "romantic, antique days";

they borrowed many techniques from Defoe (with his realistic attention to detail) and Richardson (his sentiment) and they added something novel in the emphasis given to natural (if often idealized) scenery as a means of expressing the moods of the characters. They took the internal landscapes of the mind and gave them external form.

The Gothic castle itself, that formidable place, ruinous yet an effective prison, phantasmagorically shifting its outline as ever new vaults extended from their labyrinths, scene of solitary wanderings, cut off from light and human contact, of unformulated menace and the terror of the living dead — this hold, with all its hundred names, now looms to investigators as the symbol of a neurosis; they see it as the gigantic symbol of anxiety, the dread of oppression and of the abyss, the response to the . . . insecurity of disturbed times.

(Herbert Read, "Introduction", *The Gothic Flame*)

The popularity of the Gothic rose as the impact of the Industrial Revolution increased, reflecting, symbolizing and even "explaining" the anxiety felt by those who witnessed radical changes in the world they knew. There are parallels today between the popularity of science fiction and major social changes which are now taking place. Invasions from outer space are symbolic versions of a threat to one's habitual way of life. The flying saucers carry cargoes of the terrors we rarely admit to and refuse to examine. And the historical romance is still there to satisfy those who look back to a simpler past, but it lacks the substance of its Gothic ancestors.

> The savageness of Gothic stands for wildness of thought and roughness of work, and impresses upon us the image of a race full of wolfish life, and an imagination as wild and wayward as the northern seas. The darkened air, the pile of buttresses and rugged walls uncouthly hewn out of rocks over wild moors, speak of the savageness of their massy architecture, which was rude, ponderous, stiff, sombre and depressing.
>
> (Devendra P. Varma, *The Gothic Flame*)

Admirers of Howard and Lovecraft will probably recognize the appeal of the Gothic.

The best of the Gothic novelists are Walpole, Ann Radcliffe, William Beckford, William Godwin, Matthew Gregory Lewis, Mary Shelley and Charles Maturin. Unlike the Chivalric Romances, their work is easily obtainable.

Mrs Radcliffe's books, like most other Gothics,

involved a wicked nobleman dwelling in a massive and oppressive Gothic castle, part of which was ruined. The wicked nobleman pursues and incarcerates, incarcerates and pursues the pure heroine through the labyrinthine corridors of his castle until she is finally rescued by the upright hero who is likely to be the true heir to the castle and its lands. This basic plot was, with a few exceptions, virtually the only plot of the Gothics, and the mixture was varied by its choice of supernatural events, although several spectres were always included. Ann Radcliffe is considered its greatest exponent. Here she describes her heroine's first sight of Udolpho:

> Emily gazed with melancholy awe upon the castle . . . for, though it was now lighted up by the setting sun, the Gothic greatness of its features, and its mouldering walls of dark grey stone, rendered it a gloomy and sublime object . . . The light died away on its walls, leaving a melancholy purple tint, which spread deeper and deeper as the thin vapour crept up the mountain, while the battlements above were still tipped with splendour. . . Silent, lonely, and sublime, it seemed to stand the sovereign of the scene and to frown defiance on all who dared its solitary reign. As the twilight deepened, its

features became more aweful in obscurity. . .
till its clustering towers were alone seen rising above the tops of the woods. . . The extent and darkness of these tall woods
awakened terrific images in her mind. . .
(She) soon after reached the castle gates,
where the deep tone of the portal bell. . .
increased the fearful emotions that had as-
sailed (her). . . she anxiously surveyed the
edifice; but the gloom that overspread it
allowed her to distinguish little more than. . .
the massy walls of the ramparts, and to know
that it was vast, ancient and dreary.

(*The Mysteries of Udolpho*)

This was the sort of thing which was to influence Byron, Shelley, Wordsworth, Coleridge
and de Quincey. It was to influence Mary Shelley,
Edgar Allan Poe, Bram Stoker and all those writers
whose work, via the motion picture screen, has
given the world new myths and folk-tales. It
influenced Scott, of course, and resulted in the
foundation of a lasting form of historical romance.
Directly or indirectly it influenced Lovecraft and
the *Weird Tales* writers:

. . . A certain huge, dark church . . . stood out
with especial distinctness at certain hours of
the day, and at sunset the great tower and
tapering steeple loomed blackly against the

flaming sky. It seemed to rest on especially high ground; for the grimy façade, and the obliquely seen north side with sloping roof and the tops of great pointed windows, rose boldly above the tangle of surrounding ridgepoles and chimney-pots. Peculiarly grimy and austere, it appeared to be built of stone, stained and weathered with the smoke and storms of a century or more. The style, so far as the glass could show, was the earliest experimental form of Gothic revival . . . The longer he watched the more his imagination worked, till at length he began to fancy curious things.

(Lovecraft, "The Haunter of the Dark")

Goethe, Fenimore Cooper, Dumas, Hugo, Balzac, Sue, and all the French Romantics were to be influenced by the Gothic in one way or another. Crude in themselves these tales spawned an enormous variety of work and in popular form their style and content has hardly changed at all. As Dr Varma says in *The Gothic Flame*: "The Gothic novels present no restful human shades of grey: the characters are mostly either endowed with sombre, diabolical villainy or pure angelic virtue. Interfering fathers, brutal in threats, oppress the hero or heroine into a loathed marriage; officials of the Inquisition or the characters of abbots and abbesses are imbued with fiendish cruelty, often gloating in Gothic diabolism over their tortures."

Evil monks and nuns were often central characters in the Gothics — the cowl shading the face was of particular appeal. Ruined castles, abbeys, convents, labyrinths, hidden vaults, overpowering natural scenery are standard to almost all of them. Supplying the fantastic element, perhaps unconsciously as a respectable substitute for de Sade's more outrageous developments, we find vampires, werewolves, ghosts of assorted kinds, portraits that come suddenly to life, witches' sabbats, walking corpses and, indeed, all the familiar supernatural elements beloved of Hammer films and Roger Corman. The sexual aspects, of course, are always disguised and only in Lewis's *The Monk* do they ever threaten to reveal themselves for what they are. A terror of normal sexuality is another common theme (see the quote below from John Norman, page 135). The character of Lewis's monk, Ambrosio, who changes from a blameless and pure life to one of rape, torture, murder, necromancy and incest, is unforgettable. It is, as it were, a Freudian's dream, with its emphasis on violence, slimy filth, loathsome creatures, drenching blood . . . . "Often," says the incarcerated nun Agnes, "have I sat waking found my fingers ringed with the long worms which bred in the corrupted flesh of my infant." As in many such books there is a version of the Faustian theme beloved of conservative writers of Romance. Ambrosio has sold his soul to the devil, but pays a dreadful penalty:

Ambrosio started, and expected the demon with terror . . . . The thunder ceasing to roll, a full strain of melodious music sounded in the air! At the same time the cloud disappeared, and he beheld a figure more beautiful than fancy's pencil ever drew. It was a youth seemingly scarce eighteen, the perfection of whose form and face was unrivalled. He was perfectly naked, a bright star sparkled on his forehead, two crimson wings extended themselves from his shoulders, and his silken locks were confined by a band of many-coloured fires, which shone with a brilliancy far surpassing that of precious stones. Circlets of diamonds were fastened around his arms and ankles, and in his right hand he bore a silver branch imitating myrtle. His form shone with dazzling glory: he was surrounded by clouds of rose-coloured light, and at the moment that he appeared a refreshing air breathed perfumes throughout the cavern. Ambrosio gazed upon the spirit with delight and wonder.

*

As in modern science fiction and fantasy there is very little overt eroticism in most Gothic novels and many habitual readers of Gothics, content to enjoy the hidden and somewhat morbid joys of the form, reacted against *The Monk* when it first appeared in 1796.

Maturin's *Melmoth the Wanderer*, the tale of a doomed near-immortal who lives for 150 years enjoying (or being told about) many strange adventures, is probably the longest and most ambitious of these stories and one of my favourites. Here, too, is morbid sexuality, supernatural horror and the rest, but it is crystallized and utilized to more significant effect. The narrative technique is complicated and likely to annoy the modern reader (it consists of a series of tales, each inside the other) but the character of Melmoth is perfectly described. To me he is a better character than (and the ancestor of) Roderic Usher. Possibly also he is an ancestor of Dorian Gray and Mr Hyde. The early part of this four-volume novel describes how an Englishman named Stanton pursues Melmoth, obsessed by the mystery surrounding him. He meets him, on one occasion, after visiting the theatre. . . .

When the play was over, he stood for some moments in the deserted streets. It was a beautiful moonlight night, and he saw near him a figure, whose shadow, projected half across the street (there were no flagged ways then, chains and posts were the only defence of the foot passenger), appeared to him of gigantic magnitude. He had been so long accustomed to contend with these phantoms of the imagination, that he took a kind of stubborn delight in subduing them. He walked up to the object, and observing the shadow only was magnified, and the figure was the ordinary height of a man, he approached it, and discovered the very object of his search — the man whom he had seen for a moment in Valentia, and, after a search of four years, recognized at the theatre.

"You were in quest of me?" — "I was." "Have you any thing to inquire of me?" — "Much." "Speak, then." — "This is no place." "No place! poor wretch, I am independent of time and place. Speak, if you have any thing to ask or to learn?" — "I have many things to ask, but nothing to learn, I hope, from you." "You deceive yourself, but you will be undeceived when next we meet." — "And when shall that be?" said Stanton, grasping his arm; "name your hour and your place." "The hour shall be mid-day," answered the stranger, with a horrid and unintelligible smile; "and the place shall be the bare walls of a madhouse, where you shall rise rattling in your chains, and rustling from your straw, to greet me — yet still you shall have *the curse of sanity*, and of memory. My voice shall ring in your ears till then, and the glance of these eyes shall be reflected from every object, animate or inanimate, till you behold them again." — "Is it under circumstances so horrible we are to meet again?" said Stanton, shrinking under the full-lighted blaze of those demon eyes. "I never," said the stranger, in an emphatic tone — "I *never desert my friends in misfortune*. When they are plunged in the lowest abyss of human calamity, *they are sure to be visited by me*."

Melmoth is the devil's agent, given immortality as long as he can supply new victims to his master. He visits those in distress (as Stanton is in distress according to his prophecy) offering them aid in return for their souls. But this we aren't told for hundreds of pages and it is a tribute to Maturin that he holds our attention through dozens of digressions. In Godwin, in Beckford, in Mary Shelley and Maturin, in Mrs Dacre's *Zofloya, the Diabolical Moor*, science is inextricably mixed with alchemy and scientific investigation confused with diabolism. Fundamentally writers of this type of story are against change, seeing it as dangerous and destructive; they are diametrically opposed to any form of radical utopianism even though they may often use the same kind of imaginative trappings for their stories. Melmoth's punishment for his experiments and studies is spectacular. Having lived 200 years, having failed to find one person who will agree to his proposition, Melmoth knows he must perish: "No one has ever exchanged destinies with Melmoth the Wanderer. *I have traversed the world in the search, and no one, to gain the world, would lose his own soul!*" He then dreams of his fate:

His last despairing reverted glance was fixed on the clock of eternity — the upraised black arm seemed to push forward the hand — it arrived at its period — he fell — he sunk — he blazed — he shrieked! The burning waves boomed over his sinking head, and the clock of eternity rung out its awful chime — "Room for the soul of the Wanderer!" — and the waves of the burning ocean answered, as they lashed the adamantine rock — "There is room for more!" — The Wanderer awoke.

Having wakened, the Wanderer discovers he has aged hideously and tells his visitors, "I am summoned, and must obey the summons — my master has other work for me! When a meteor blazes in your atmosphere — when a comet pursues its burning path towards the sun — look up, and perhaps you may think of the spirit condemned to guide the blazing and erratic orb." He warns them that if they watch him leave the house "your lives will be the forfeit of your desperate curiosity. For the same stake I risked more than life — and lost it!" He leaves and terrible shrieks are heard from the nearby cliffs overlooking the sea, indescribable sounds are heard all night over the surrounding countryside. In the morning there is only one trace of the Wanderer on the rocks above the sea — his handkerchief.

Melmoth the Wanderer was published in 1820. Robert Spector in his introduction to *Seven Masterpieces of Gothic Horror* has this to say: "*Melmoth the Wanderer* is a Faust story that begins in contemporary Ireland but re-creates the adventures of John Melmoth, who has lived since the seventeenth century through a pact with the devil. Through six episodes of terror, Maturin creates the experiences of modern anguish. Maturin combines the myths of Faust and the Wandering Jew with all the horrible episodes of the Gothic romances, and yet he never depends on blood and gore for his effects. What Maturin does is to probe the psychological depths of fear, and, in doing so, he was a little ahead of his audience. Although

Melmoth has come to be regarded by many as the masterpiece of terror fiction, it attracted little attention* until psychological Gothicists like Poe and the French Romantics resurrected it some years later."

Throughout this long book Melmoth can also be seen as the Faceless Man of our dreams, the unknown aspect of ourselves which is symbolized as well in the figure of the cowled monk or the shadowy, omniscient spectre. He appears in many modern fantasy tales — Leiber's Sheelba of the Eyeless Face in the "Gray Mouser" stories, Tolkien's faceless villain in *The Lord of the Rings*, Poul Anderson's Odin in *The Broken Sword*, even Alfred Bester's Burning Man in *Tiger! Tiger!* There is a link, too, perhaps, between the unknown aspect and the "evil" aspect of ourselves in that we sense the presence of the unknown aspect and fear it, therefore judging it "evil". Robert Louis Stevenson might have experienced such a process and in *Dr Jekyll and Mr Hyde* (1886), inspired by fever-dreams and nightmares during a bad illness, produced a new variant on the Faust-character as Jekyll slowly becomes dominated by Hyde. *The Picture of Dorian Gray* (1891) is another development of the theme. Maturin was an ancestor of Wilde's and Wilde changed his name to Sebastian

---

*See Alethea Hayter's introduction to the current Penguin edition for a slightly different account of the book's success.

Melmoth when he came out of prison and went to live in Dieppe.

The doomed hero, bound to destroy himself and those he loves, is one of the oldest character-types in literature. Byron saw himself in this role, to the discomfort of his friends and family, and by acting it out helped to foster it in Romantic literature. A good many successful rock and roll performers play a similar role and, as often as not, are destroyed by it, thus giving a form of authenticity to the myth. Recent hero-villains in fantastic fiction have been Mervyn Peake's Steerpike in the *Gormenghast* books, Anderson's Scafloc in *The Broken Sword*, T. H. White's Lancelot in *The Once and Future King* and Jane Gaskell's Zerd in *The Serpent*. Bram Stoker's *Dracula* (1897) is, of course, another variation. Here vampirism is the strongest element in the story, but Count Dracula's lust for blood is almost identical to the lust for virtuous women which marked his predecessors. Faust desired to have and corrupt Margaret, just as dozens of later "demon-lovers" like Radcliffe's Schedoni, Ambrosio and, in real life, Byron and de Sade claimed to pursue innocence solely to destroy it. This peculiar ambition apparently possessed a lot of the great hero-villains. It even seemed to be the secret of their attraction for those refined middle-class women who made up the greatest part of the

Gothic's readership and who still comprise the main audience for that degenerated thing, the "Gothic Romance" published by Harlequin and Mills & Boon in huge numbers.

It would be refreshing, however, to see a few more good hero-villains in modern epic fantasy. Even better would be some full-blooded heroine-villainesses! Their presence might improve a form which is already showing signs of sterility.

2

The Exotic Landscape

With the sight of those lofty walls and the scent
of the dry sweet sage there rushed over me a
strange feeling that *Riders of the Purple Sage*
was true. My dream people of romance had
really lived there once upon a time. I climbed
high upon the huge stones where Fay Larkin
once had glided with swift sure steps, and I
entered the musty cliff-dwellings, and called
out to hear the weird, sonorous echoes, and I
wandered through the thickets and upon the
grassy spruce-shaded benches, never for a moment free of the story I had conceived there.
Something of awe and sadness abided with me.
Surprise Valley seemed a part of my past, my
dreams, my very self. I left it, haunted by its
loneliness and silence and beauty, by the story
it had given me.

    Zane Grey, *Tales of Lonely Trails*, 1922

An intrinsic part of the epic fantasy is exotic
landscape. This dream-scenery is fundamental to
the success of any romantic work, from Walpole to
Ballard; it is often the substance of such work, and

no matter how well drawn their characters or good their language writers will appeal to the dedicated reader of romance according to the skill by which they evoke settings, whether natural or invented. Their work may be judged not by normal criteria but by the "power" of their imagery and by what extent their writing evokes that "power", whether they are trying to convey "wildness", "strangeness" or "charm"; whether, like Melville, Ballard, Juenger, Patrick White or Alejo Carpentier, they transform their images into intense personal metaphors or, like Bunyan, give us simple allegory:

> As I walked through the wilderness of this world, I lighted on a certain place where was a den, and laid me down to sleep; and as I slept, I dreamed a dream. I dreamed, and behold, I saw a man clothed with rags standing in a certain place, a book in his hand, and a great burden on his back. . . .
>
> *The Pilgrim's Progress*, 1678

The English sf "disaster story" is an obvious attempt by authors to remould landscapes to their own literary ends and the device of world-catastrophe proves very useful to them. The central appeal in such books is the landscape, which can be harsh or comfortable, depending on the author's intentions, though often the weight of sf rationalization — "logical" explication — will collapse the structure and leave only a fragment of the original conception behind, partly because matter-of-fact language and lyrical imagery rarely work to support one another. I discuss elsewhere the appeal of the rural English landscape, the landscape of lost innocence (*à la* Tolkien and his imitators) which derives, I suspect, from the tradition of the pastoral romance (*Arcadia* etc.) through 19th-century writers like Borrow, and has modern exponents as varied as R. F. Delderfield and Miss Read, but little link with Ann Radcliffe, Clara Reeve, Scott, the Brontës, Stevenson or, for instance, Raymond Chandler, all of whom in different ways imposed an idiosyncratic vision on their scenery. Occasionally, of course, Tolkien manages a romantic evocation or two, passages which are admired by many contemporary readers who do not otherwise enjoy him. But Tolkien's enormous success could easily be in direct relation to the extent to which the elements of romance are absent from his narrative. As Fritz Leiber — probably America's leading living fantast — wrote in a letter to Lin Carter:

There's no arguing that a vast number of people . . . are tremendously and enduringly enthusiastic about Tolkien's trilogy, yet I do meet quite a few whose reactions are much like my own. We almost always start with

"The ents are great! Oh boy, yes. And that first part of the quest with the black riders in the distance and Strider a mystery — that's great, too. And yes, the first appearance of the Nazgul and the Balrog . . ." At about which point the silence begins and we search our memories and look at each other rather guiltily — exciting things *should* spring to mind, but they don't . . . He's not interested in women and he's not really interested in the villains unless they're just miserable sneaks, bullies and resentful cowards like Gollum . . . Tolkien (so unlike Eddison) does not explore and even seems uninterested in exploring the mentality and consciousness and inner life of his chief villains.

1969, quoted in *Imaginary Worlds*
by Lin Carter, 1973

A writer of fantasy must be judged by the level of inventive intensity at which he or she works. Allegory can be nonexistent but a certain amount of conscious metaphor is always there. The writer who follows such originals without understanding this produces work which is at best superficially entertaining and at worst meaningless on any level — generic dross doing nothing to revitalize the form from which it borrows. A writer's work tends to last in direct ratio to the degree of originality and vitality put into it. Although William Morris is doubtless the originator of the story set in an imaginary land where the supernatural is a fact of life, he borrowed so heavily from Nordic and mediaeval models, in prose, imagery and even characters, that his later writing has little appeal to the modern reader. In his early short prose romances published in the *Oxford and Cambridge Magazine* in 1856 he showed an enthusiasm and vigour generally lacking in his mature work:

> I dreamed once, that four men sat by the winter fire talking and telling tales, in a house that the wind howled around.
>
> And one of them, the eldest, said: "When I was a boy, before you came to this land, that bar of red sand rock, which makes a fall in our river, had only just been formed; for it used to stand above the river in a great cliff, tunnelled by a cave about midway between the green-growing grass and the green-flowing river; and it fell one night, when you had not yet come to this land, no, nor your fathers."
>
> *The Dream*

By the end of his life the level of his description was, at its best, usually of this sort:

> It is told that there was once a mighty river which ran south into the sea, and at the

mouth thereof was a great and rich city, which had been builded and had waxed and thriven because of the great and most excellent haven which the river aforesaid made where it fell into the sea, and now it was like looking at a huge wood of barked and smoothened fir-trees when one saw the masts of the ships that lay in the said haven.

The Sundering Flood, 1898

The image itself — masts of ships like a forest — is not original and is further marred by the lifeless, imitative prose. A somewhat better writer and the first to follow Morris's example of setting his stories in exotic, invented lands was Lord Dunsany who learned much from Wilde and the aesthetes, from Irish folklorists, poets and dramatists like Yeats and Synge. His prose and his invention are often witty, paradoxical, deriving in part from Oriental fantasies such as those of Beckford, Moore and Burton, and possibly from Doughty's Arabian reminiscences. Like most fantasts he owed a good deal to Thomas de Quincey and Edgar Allan Poe, in both technique and style. De Quincey gives us:

The unimaginable horror which these dreams of oriental imagery and mythological tortures impressed upon me . . . I was stared at, hooted at, grinned at, chattered at, by monkeys, by paroquets, by cockatoos. I ran into pagodas, and was fixed for centuries at the summit, or in secret rooms; I was the idol; I was the priest; I was sacrificed . . . I came suddenly upon Isis and Osiris: I had done a deed, they said, which the ibis and the crocodile trembled at. Thousands of years I lived and was buried in stone coffins, with mummies and sphinxes, in narrow chambers at the heart of eternal pyramids. I was kissed, with cancerous kisses, by crocodiles, and was laid, confounded with all unutterable abortions, amongst reeds and Nilotic mud.

Confessions of an English Opium Eater, 1822

While from Poe we have the story of "Eleanora" (1840), its narrator dreaming of a past reality more powerful than his present; and of a River of Silence and a Valley of the Many-Coloured Grass:

And, here and there, in groves about this grass, like a wilderness of dreams, sprang up fantastic trees, whose tall slender stems stood not upright, but slanted gracefully towards the light that peered at noon-day into the centre of the valley. Their bark was speckled with the vivid alternate splendour of ebony and silver; and was smoother than all save the cheeks of Eleanora; so that but for the brilliant green of the huge leaves that spread from their summits in long, tremulous lines, dallying with the zephyrs, one might have fancied them giant serpents of Syria doing homage to their sovereign the Sun.

Or from "Shadow — a Parable":

Over some flasks of the red Chian wine, within the walls of a noble hall, in a dim city called Ptolemais, we sat, at night, a company of seven. And to our chamber there was no entrance save by a lofty door of brass: and the door was fashioned by the artisan Corianos, and, being of rare workmanship, was fastened from within. Black draperies, likewise, in the gloomy room, shut out from our view the moon, the lurid stars, and the peopleless streets — but the boding and the memory of Evil, they would not be so excluded.

Dunsany gradually excluded the smell of death as well as the memory of Evil from almost everything he wrote but added humour. The following echoes Poe, yet it is the work of a very different kind of imagination:

Where the great plain of Tarphet runs up, as the sea in estuaries, among the Cyresian mountains, there stood long since the city of Merimna well-nigh among the shadows of the crags. I have never seen a city in the world so beautiful as Merimna seemed to me when first I dreamed of it. It was a marvel of spires and figures of bronze, and marble fountains, and trophies of fabulous wars, and broad streets given over wholly to the Beautiful.

The Sword of Welleran, 1908

In fact it is much more reminiscent of Wilde in tone. Here is Wilde:

In the fourth month we reached the city of Illel. It was night time when we came to the grove that is outside the walls, and the air was sultry, for the Moon was travelling in Scorpion. We took the ripe pomegranates from the trees, and brake them, and drank their sweet juices. Then we lay down on our carpets and waited for the dawn. And at dawn we rose and knocked at the gate of the city. It was wrought out of red bronze, and carved with sea-dragons and dragons that have wings. The guards looked down from the battlements and asked us our business.

"The Fisherman and his Soul", 1888

As with so much fantastic literature the inspiration is from romantic poetry, from *Kubla Khan*, from *Lalla Rookh*, from Keats, from Shelley, from Tennyson and Swinburne. Unfortunately only rarely does the prose ever come to match the best of the poetry. Often the prose is little more than a mindless imitation of the euphonious aspects of the verse which, lacking the substance of the original, takes on the aspect of a mute attempting desperately to sing a Mozart song by mouthing an approximation of the sounds he has heard. All the nonsensical archaicisms and meaningless sonority, borrowed from Gothic and Pre-Raphaelite writers used, as often as not, to colour up an essentially lifeless and unimaginative narrative, tends to discredit those few writers, like William Hope Hodgson, who instil vigour and fresh meaning into their language. Hodgson's huge book, which is more nearly a visionary work in the manner of Bunyan than it is a conceit in the manner of Dunsany, is *The Night Land* (1912) (most recently paperbacked in a poorly edited and garbled text):

And afar down the gorge, I did see the shinings of strange fires, faint and a great way off. And so was I come at last to the bottom of the Mighty Slope. Yet the gorge also to go downward, but not so great.

And presently I did go forward again; and so did open the point of the rocks, as the sailors do say. And I saw now that there gushed forth a great blue flame from the earth; and the mighty rocks stood about it, as that they were olden giants grouped there to some strange service.

And concerning this flame I was not over-much astonished in my Reason: for it had seemed to me as I drew anigh, that the fire and the sound should be made by the roaring and whistling of a burning gas that did issue forth among the rocks. Yet, truly, though it did be a natural matter, it was yet a wondrous sight, and set amazement on my senses; for the flame did dance, and sway whitherward mon-strously, and sometimes did seem that it dropt so low as an hundred feet, and afterward went upward with a vast roaring unto the utter height, and did stand mighty and blaz-ing, maybe a full thousand feet, so that the far side of the gorge was lit, and surely it was seven great miles off or more; but yet did show plain and wondrous. And the light did show me the flank of the mountain, that made the right hand side of the Gorge, to go up measure-less into the night.

This is archaism used to much livelier effect than Morris's. While the aesthetes were giving us their ornamental style of romance, Kipling was producing, in his Mowgli stories in particular, a style which was to influence a great many of his contemporaries and offer a prevailing voice in the next century. Told simply, yet lyrically, his jungle stories were to influence many American writers, among them Edgar Rice Burroughs whose first fiction was a fantastic romance set on Mars borrowed from Edwin Lester Arnold and Pope's *Journey to Mars* (1894) and in style influenced (perhaps at a stage or two removed) by Kipling and Jack London (whose own *Call of the Wild* owes a great deal to Kipling). This laconic as opposed to lyrical romanticism, with admiration of the naïve outsider, the primitive — the unrepressed wish-fulfilment "noble savage" of Victorian fiction — was to be the dominant voice in science fiction and fantasy until relatively recently. Yet it still depended on landscape for much of its appeal. Burroughs created a Mars which was to stimulate the imaginations of a diversity of science fiction writers from Leigh Brackett to Ray Bradbury for the next fifty years:

> The quiet of the tomb lay upon the mysterious valley of death, crouching deep in its warm nest within the sunken area at the south pole of the dying planet. In the far distance the Golden Cliffs raised their mighty barrier faces far into the starlit heavens, the precious metals and scintillating jewels that composed them sparkling in the brilliant light of Mars's two gorgeous moons.
>
> At my back was the forest, pruned and trimmed like the sward to parklike symmetry by the browsing of the ghoulish plant men.

Before me lay the Lost Sea of Korus, while farther on I caught the shimmering ribbon of Iss, the River of Mystery, where it would rush out from beneath the Golden Cliffs to empty into Korus, to which for countless ages had been borne the deluded and unhappy Martians of the outer world upon the voluntary pilgrimage to this false heaven.

The Gods of Mars, 1918

Echoes of the Gothic relish for decaying landscape and ruins abound in Burroughs. His "dead sea-bottoms" set the pattern for a fictional Mars, a dying culture on a world almost wholly desert, which many writers were loath to give up, inventing future Earths or planets orbiting faraway stars, rather than relinquish such potent images. Burroughs was much influenced by H. Rider Haggard, especially in his Tarzan novels (She-Who-Must-Be-Obeyed and La of Opar are virtually twin sisters), but the American writer to learn most from Haggard and, in my opinion, write better romances, was Abraham Merritt who produced comparatively little work, some of it virtually without any human viewpoint or dramatic tension, but the majority very much linking grotesque and fantastical scenery with a strong adventure element:

There was something about that immense ebon citadel that struck me with the same sense of fore-knowledge that I had felt when I had ridden into the ruins of the Gobi oasis. Also I thought it looked like that city of Dis which Dante had glimpsed in Hades. And its antiquity hung over it like a sable garment.

Then I saw that Nansur was broken. Between the arch that winged from the side on which we stood and the arch that swept up and out from the side of the black citadel, there was a gap. It was as though a gigantic hammer had been swung down on the soaring bow, shattering it at its center. I thought of Bifrost Bridge over which the Valkyries rode, bearing souls of the warriors to Valhalla; and I thought it had been as great blasphemy to have broken Nansur Bridge as it would have been to have broken Bifrost.

Dwellers in the Mirage, 1932

E. R. Eddison, the British author of *The Worm Ouroboros*, was perhaps the last to reflect the atmosphere of the previous generation's love for the archaic and the bizarre. He is thought by many to represent the apotheosis of a tradition, a much more witty and original writer than Morris, a rather more original inventor of landscape than Dunsany. . . .

Juss walked long in the doubtful light, troubled at heart . . . The glimmer of the lamps mingled with his dreams and his dreams with it, so that scarce he wist whether asleep or waking he beheld the walls of the bedchamber, dispart in sunder, disclosing a prospect of vast paths of moonlight, and a solitary mountain peak standing naked out of a sea of cloud that gleamed white beneath the moon. It seemed to him that the power of flight was upon him, and that he flew to that mountain and hung in air beholding it near at hand, and a circle as the appearance of fire round about it, and on the summit of the mountain the likeness of a bur or citadel of brass that was green with eld and surface-battered by the frosts and winds of ages. On the battlements was the appearance of a great company both men and women, never still, now walking on the wall with hands lifted up as in supplication to the crystal lamps of heaven, now flinging themselves on their knees or leaning against the brazen battlements to bury their faces in their hands, or standing at gaze as night-walkers gazing into the void. Some seemed men of war, and some great courtiers by their costly apparel, rulers and kings and kings' daughters, grave bearded counsellors, youths and maidens and crowned queens. And when they went and when they stood, and when they seemed to cry aloud bitterly, all was noiseless even as the tomb, and the faces of those mourners pallid as a dead corpse is pallid.

The Worm Ouroboros, 1926

It is a feature of the work of many romantic writers that they distance themselves in this way. Scott in his *Journal* remarks:

I saw the poor child's funeral from a distance. Ah, that Distance! What a magician for conjuring up scenes of joy or sorrow, smoothing all asperities, reconciling all incongruities, veiling all absurdness, softening every coarseness, doubling every effect by the influence of the imagination.

It is probably no coincidence that the majority of writers best known as fantasts are introverted, reclusive, misanthropic, or that a strong vein of misogynism has built itself into the conventions of the genre over the years, so that women are unbelievably beautiful goddesses, treacherous jades or silly slave-girls. Much fantasy is characteristically bachelor-fiction largely written and read by that section of the community. Certainly H. P. Lovecraft's unstable childhood might have turned anyone peculiar and made them seek escape in Romance. An aggressive, neurotic personality, Lovecraft came under the influence of Poe, Dunsany and the imaginative writers of the Munsey pulp magazines and produced some of the most powerful infantile pathological imagery and some of the most astonishingly awful prose ever to gain popularity, yet his early work, written primarily in homage to Dunsany, from whom he borrowed the idea of an invented pantheon of gods, is lighter in touch and almost completely lacking in the morbid imagery of his more successful horror stories in which death, idealism, lust and terror of sexual intercourse are constantly associated in prose which becomes increasingly confused as the author's embattled psyche received wound after wound and he regressed into an attitude of permanent defensiveness. The longest example of this Dunsany phase is *The Dream Quest of Unknown Kadath* (published in book form, 1955).

Clark Ashton Smith was another American recluse who wrote very much under the influence of Poe and Dunsany. His main career as a writer of short stories, primarily for *Weird Tales*, the pulp which published the bulk of American fantastic fiction from 1923 to 1954, lasted for only six years, in which time he produced nearly a hundred stories, most of them set in invented worlds of the remote past or remote future, some of them on distant planets, all of them exotic. The stories were written with such intensity and control that it is reasonable to guess that Smith burned himself out, perhaps entering a period of depression from which he never completely recovered. Smith's enthusiasm for the Romantics was more literary than most of his contemporaries. He translated Baudelaire and wrote disciplined poetry himself. His prose contains a vitality rarely apparent in this kind of fiction and there is very frequently a strong vein of irony which was to mark the work of a later writer, Fritz Leiber. In Smith intelligence and a genuine love of language, an almost playful relish for the exotic, a carelessness of spirit, in great contrast to the obsessive aggression of Lovecraft, make his work more palatable to me. Just as "distanced", just as suspicious of the world, particularly women, just as morbid in many ways, Smith's stories lack the neurotic drone of writers like Lovecraft, and contain a good deal of ordinary humour. For me, it is his tone which makes him readable where Lovecraft is not:

Toward night, as the sun declined above that tumultuous ebon ocean, it seemed that a great bank of thunder-cloud arose from the west, long and low-lying at first, but surging rapidly skyward with the mountainous domes. Ever higher it loomed, revealing the menace as of piled cliffs and somber, awful seascapes; but its form changed not in the fashion of clouds; and Yadar knew it at last for an island bulking far aloft in the long-rayed sunset. From it a shadow was thrown for leagues, darkening still more the sable waters, as if with the fall of untimely night; and in the shadow the foam-crests flashing upon hidden reefs were white as the bared teeth of death. And Yadar needed not the shrill frightened cries of his companions to tell him that this was the terrible Isle of Naat.

"Necromancy in Naat", 1936, from *Lost Worlds*

Smith was able to combine rapid action with his descriptions, as Stevenson often did, his landscapes actually contributing to his story's dynamic. In this he had something in common with Robert E. Howard, another reclusive young man who wrote at an enormous rate for a few years before killing himself when his mother's death evidently coincided with a bout of depression resulting from creative exhaustion. Howard wrote pulp adventure stories of every kind, for every market he could find, but his real love was for supernatural adventure and he brought a brash, tough element to the epic fantasy which did as much to change the course of the American school away from precious writing and static imagery as Hammett, Chandler and the *Black Mask* pulp writers were to change the course of American detective fiction. Howard had no literary ambitions but possessed a vitality his followers never captured. His influences were other pulp writers like Edgar Rice Burroughs, Talbot Mundy, Harold Lamb, Francis Terhune, Abraham Merritt, and his descriptions of interiors and landscapes though rarely very original were intrinsic to the story he was telling. In his Conan stories and his Solomon Kane stories, much more directly influenced by historical novelists in the tradition of Scott and Stevenson, Howard unconsciously produced a remarriage of Gothic and Chivalric traditions in a popular idiom:

The two hosts confronted each other across a wide, shallow valley, with rugged cliffs, and a shallow stream winding through masses of reeds and willows down the middle of the vale. The camp-followers of both hosts came down to this stream for water, and shouted insults and hurled stones across at one another. The last glints of the sun shone on the golden banner of Nemedia with the scarlet dragon, unfurled in the breeze above the pavilion of King Tarascus on an eminence near the eastern cliffs. But the shadow of the western cliffs fell like a vast purple pall across the tents and the army of Aquilonia, and upon the black banner with its golden lion that floated above King Conan's pavilion.

Conan the Conqueror, 1936

Sadly the vitality of the original Conan stories has not been reproduced in the imitations (including films) since done by a variety of hands, and Howard's virtues (as a synthesist if nothing else) are likely to be ignored as exploitative publishers encourage further imitations and republish every piece of mediocre work Howard ever wrote. The best of his imitators were contemporaries, who were writing under the same influences.

The movie versions of Conan borrow as many elements from the rest of the genre as they do from Howard, but for me they remain inferior in every way to the originals. The *Star Wars* movies, deriving plot materials from comic books and, among others, Italian Westerns, have had as much influence on these sword-and-sorcery films as anything else. *Hawk the Slayer*, *The Sword and the Sorcerer* and most of the others have a simple revenge motif as their main dynamic, while almost all have mysteriously missing relatives as the object of a quest. The repetitiveness of the clichés says a great deal, in my view, about the caution and lack of creative originality which currently infects the film business. The simple-minded machismo of the movie Conan is a little like that of the movie Tarzan. All potential is lost. A good director, surely, could do more with the material, rather than less, but the threatened schoolboys who dominate Hollywood seem only too eager to indulge their fifth-rate fantasies of male violence, be it via *Rambo*, *Death Wish* or *Conan* himself. We have witnessed a deterioration from the crude, powerful prose of Howard, through the increasingly badly-done comic strip versions, to the feebleness of the movies. The magic fades, its real achievements going unrecognized. One longs for a good film version, say, of Fafhrd and the Gray Mouser, which conceivably might contain dialogue which grown-up actors would not be ashamed to speak!

Having no familiarity with Conan at first, influenced by Eddison and Cabell, Fritz Leiber began to publish his Fafhrd and Gray Mouser stories in a short-lived pulp magazine which had ambitions where fantasy was concerned similar to those *Black Mask* had for thrillers. *Unknown* was edited by John W. Campbell, editor of *Astounding Science Fiction*, and was best known for bringing a patina of laconic credibility or "realism" to the fantastic story.

During both world wars much less exotic fantasy was published (and presumably written). Romance had to disguise itself as realism if it was to keep an audience. With the Romantic Revival it had been able to flourish again for a time in its own terms, to disappear for a few decades until the 1960s when public taste again "allowed" it — i.e. when there was a fresh commercial market which publishers were willing to satisfy. There seemed to be a sharp decline in popular imaginative fantasy around 1914, rising gradually in the mid-twenties and declining again by around 1940, suggesting that during a world war readers have more urgent matters to hold their attention, more important facts to sentimentalize.

Unknown was a magazine for its time when it began in the late thirties and continued into the early war years, publishing some of the most literate popular fantasy ever to appear. Leiber's work was much more evidently romantic than, for instance, Anthony Boucher's (who satirized the werewolf myth in *The Compleat Werewolf*). The majority of *Unknown* writers debunked mythology, folklore and the horror genre. Leiber's Gray Mouser stories were published largely because the characters were more human and "realistic" than any previous characters in this kind of fiction. But Leiber relied as heavily as his predecessors on landscape to create his effects. One story, "The Bleak Shore", was almost as wholly imagist as, say, Stevenson's "The Merry Men". His first Fafhrd and Mouser story was "Adept's Gambit" and here is a characteristic piece of description:

So they crossed the snowy Lebanons and stole three camels, virtuously choosing to rob a rich landlord who made his tenants milk rocks and sow the shores of the Dead Sea, for it was unwise to approach the Gossiper of the Gods with an overly dirty conscience. After seven days of pitching and tossing across the desert, furnace days that made Fafhrd curse Muspelheim's fire gods, in whom he did not believe, they reached the Sand Combers and the Great Sand Whirlpools, and warily slipping past them while they were only lazily twirling, climbed the Rocky Islet. The city-loving Mouser ranted at Ningauble's preference for "a godforsaken hole in the desert", although he suspected that the Newsmonger and his agents came and went by a more hospitable road than the one provided for visitors, and although he knew as well as Fafhrd that the Snarer of Rumors (especially the false, which are the more valuable) must live as close to India and the infinite garden lands of the Yellow Men as to barbaric Britain and marching Rome, as close to the heaven-steaming trans-Ethiopian jungle as to the mystery of lonely tablelands and star-scraping mountains beyond the Caspian Sea.

Although it owes a good deal perhaps to Cabell, it is vastly superior writing to that of Howard or Lovecraft and is marked by Leiber's humane sense of humour. Fletcher Pratt, a collaborator with

L. Sprague de Camp in a remarkably funny series of spoofs for *Unknown*, deriving much inspiration from Mark Twain's *A Connecticut Yankee in King Arthur's Court* (1889), admitted the influence of Dunsany as cheerfully as Lovecraft, but his *The Well of the Unicorn* (1948), though one of the very best examples of epic fantasy, bears little trace of any stylistic influences from Pre-Raphaelitism or the Celtic Twilight. It is written in a good, direct style which, like Leiber and Howard, lacks the "distance" characteristic of the majority of writers before this time and anticipating in this *The Lord of the Rings* for, if it has virtues, it is also remarkable for its failure to employ any form of invented landscape. Its world is Nordic and familiar. The author has no great relish for descriptive writing even of the sort used by Howard. The best we get from Pratt is:

> The wind had risen during the night and under a grey sky now carried whorls of snow streaming past the windows.

It became unfashionable, even unrespectable, to employ ecstatic language in all but the most lurid of pulps and it was to these that the unrepentant romantics looked for publication in the forties and fifties: *Planet Stories* which ran Leigh Brackett's wonderful Eric John Stark stories, *Thrilling Wonder Stories* and *Startling Stories* with Charles

Harness. Other shorter-lived magazines featured the occasional Howard pastiche, some Cordwainer Smith, a Leiber story; Jack Vance's *The Dying Earth* was published in a small edition in 1950, Poul Anderson's fine *The Broken Sword* was published in relative obscurity in 1954, but it was not until the mid-sixties with the advent of a new, frankly romantic school of sf and fantasy writers associated with the so-called sf new wave that the American magazines were to see a strong revival of public interest in fiction depending more for its success on witty or lyrical writing and evocative landscapes than on "ideas", rationalism and laconic prose. With the renewed success of Burroughs, the cult of Tolkien, the emergence of writers like Zelazny, Delany, Lafferty and Ellison, the tone of generic fantasy (including sf) began to change as a substantial readership developed amongst young people throughout the West. Romantic and mystical writers were revived, together with half-forgotten painters and poets: De Quincey's followers in the so-called drug-culture became legion. A new vogue for the Pre-Raphaelites, for the Aesthetes, the Symbolists, began. Today, however, the exotic landscape seems to be predominantly the province of a new school of commercial artists, and authors writing in imitation of the "discovered" masters like Dunsany and Howard are often content to use prefabricated landscapes. To my knowledge only a few writers now produce epic fantasy which makes conscious literary use of exotic landscape. One of these, M. John Harrison, began experimenting with the form in his *The Pastel City*. His dying world of the far future derives a fair bit from Smith and Vance, owes a trifle to Ballard, but his landscapes illuminate a personal vision:

> Dawn broke yellow and black like an omen over the Cobalt-mere, where isolated wreaths of night-mist still hung over the dark, smooth water. From the eyots and reed-beds, fowl cackled: dimly sensing the coming winter, they were gathering in great multicoloured drifts on the surface of the lake, slow migratory urges building to a climax in ten thousand small, dreary skulls.
>
> *The Pastel City*, 1971

Like Leiber, Harrison is a long way from the oral tradition which so influenced Dunsany, but very much in the literary tradition of Stevenson, and none the worse for that. Moreover, Harrison has developed his work in recent years to arrive at his own specialized kind of fantasy — where the epic element exists only in backgrounds, in memories, in ruins, in ancient landscapes — and as the *subject matter* of the story itself. He concentrates on the lives of his characters, on the images of their old and threadbare world, on the scenery. What violence is permitted in his stories is shown always as useless, seedy, misconceived, the last resort of despairing fools. Landscape is of paramount importance to Harrison; the landscapes of Viriconium, his antique city, are an indivisible part of the personalities who occupy them. One is reflected in the other. They might even be the same. *A Storm of Wings* (1979) was the second Viriconium book and another advance into Harrison's individual territory. But it was not until *In Viriconium* (1982) that he seemed to break almost completely with any earlier formal influences:

The death and defection of his only allies left him alone in a place he hardly recognised. In one night the plague zone had extended its boundaries by two miles, perhaps three. The High City had succumbed at last. Later he was to write:

"A quiet shabbiness seemed to have descended unnoticed on the squares and avenues. Waste paper blew round my legs as I crossed the empty perspectives of the Atteline Way; the bowls of the everlasting fountains at Delpine Square were dry and dust-filled, the flagstones slippery with birdlime underfoot; insects circled and fell in the orange lamplight along the Camine Auriale. The plague had penetrated everywhere. All evening the salons and drawing rooms of the High City had been haunted by silences, pauses, *faux pas*: if anyone heard me when I flung myself exhausted against some well-known front door to get my breath it was only as another intrusion, a harsh, lonely sound which relieved briefly the stultified conversation, the unending dinner with its lukewarm sauces and overcooked mutton, or the curiously flat tone of the visiting violinist (who subsequently shook his instrument and complained, 'I find the ambience rather *unsympathetic* tonight').

"This psychological disorder of the city was reflected in a new disorder of its streets. It was a city I knew and yet I could not find my way about it. . . ."

Harrison's fantasies increasingly reflect his concern with the origins of our imaginings and why we should need (or want) to create fables and mythologies. In this he shares something in common with a number of modern writers, including Ursula K. Le Guin (see, for instance, *Threshold*, 1980), Robert Holdstock (*Mythago Wood*, 1984) and, as ever, J. G. Ballard who, in this respect, has been an enormous influence on the younger generation of fantasts. Most of Ballard's books deal with our relationship to the natural world and the myths we derive from it (*The Drowned World*, 1962, *The Terminal Beach*, 1964, *High Rise*, 1975 and even *Empire of the Sun*, 1984, display this obsession) and while he has not produced anything remotely like an epic fantasy he has been an excellent model for the best of those who have.

Thoracic Drop. The spinal landscape, revealed at the level of T-12, is that of the porous rock-towers of Tenerife, and of the native of the Canaries, Oscar Dominguez, who created the technique of decalcomania and so exposed the first spinal landscape. The clinker-like rock-towers, suspended above the silent swamp, create an impression of profound anguish. The inhospitability of this mineral world, with its inorganic growths, is relieved only by the balloons flying in the clear sky. They are painted with names: Jackie, Lee Harvey, Malcolm. In the mirror of this swamp there are no reflections. Here, time makes no concessions.

"The Assassination Weapon", 1966

Gene Wolfe, too, has an intellectual fascination with his subject matter, which does not in any way diminish his narrative gift. Of all the writers mentioned, he seems happiest in the long form, but he, too, places great importance on landscape. Wolfe's elegant, deceptively simple and sometimes beautifully ironic style, combined with the originality of his imagination and his outstanding ability as a story teller, makes him one of the very best of the generation of fantasts who have made their names in the '70s and '80s.

At one point, only slightly less than halfway down, the line of the fault had coincided with the tiled wall of some great building, so that the windy path I trod slashed across it. What the design was those tiles traced, I never knew; as I descended the cliff I was too near to see it, and when I reached the base at last it was too high for me to discern, lost in the shifting mists of the falling river. Yet as I walked, I saw it as an insect may be said to see the face in a portrait over whose surface it creeps. The tiles were of many shapes, though they fit together so closely, and at first I thought them representations of birds, lizards, fish and suchlike creatures, all inter-locked in the grip of life. Now I feel that this was not so, that they were instead the shapes of a geometry I failed to comprehend, dia-grams so complex that the living forms seemed to appear in them as the forms of actual animals appear from the intricate geometries of complex molecules.

The Sword of the Lictor, 1982

Even that enjoyable comic spoof of the Sword and Sorcery genre, Terry Pratchett's *The Colour of Magic* (1983), continues to place strong emphasis on landscape, as here:

On either side of him two glittering curtains of water hurled towards infinity as the sea swept around the island on its way to the long fall. A hundred yards below the wizard the largest sea salmon he had ever seen flicked itself out of the foam in a wild, jerky and ultimately hopeless leap. Then it fell back, over and over, in the golden under-world light.

Huge shadows grew out of that light like pillars supporting the roof of the universe. Hundreds of miles below him the wizard made out the shape of something, the edge of something—

Like those curious little pictures where the silhouette of an ornate glass suddenly becomes the outline of two faces, the scene beneath him flipped into a whole, new, terrifying perspective. Because down there was the head of an elephant as big as a reasonably-sized continent. One mighty tusk cut like a mountain against the golden light, trailing a widening shadow towards the stars. The head was slightly tilted, and a huge ruby eye might almost have been a red supergiant that had managed to shine at noonday.

Below the elephant —

Rincewind swallowed and tried not to think —

Below the elephant there was nothing but the distant, painful disc of the sun. And, sweeping slowly past it, was something that for all its city-sized scales, its crater-pocks, its lunar cragginess, was indubitably a flipper.

The inseparability between human beings and their myths is as constant a theme in epic fantasy as is our oneness with nature. Many of the writers emphasize the existence of a deep bond between humans and their world. It is the persistent element in a large proportion of modern work. Here is Patricia A. McKillip:

He left the City of Circles that evening and spent days and nights he did not count, hidden from the world and almost from himself, within the land-law of Herun. He drifted shapelessly in the mists, seeped down into the still, dangerous marshlands, and felt the morning frost silver his face as it hardened over mud and reeds and tough marsh grasses. He cried a marsh bird's lonely cry and stared at the stars out of an expressionless slab of stone.

He roamed through the low hills, linking his mind to rocks, trees, rivulets, searching into the rich mines of iron and copper and precious stones the hills kept enclosed within themselves. He spun tendrils of thought into a vast web across the dormant fields and lush, misty pastureland, linking himself to the stubble of dead roots, frozen furrows, and tangled grasses the sheep fed on. The gentleness of the land reminded him of Hed, but there was a dark, restless force in it that had reared up in the shapes of tors and monoliths.

Harpist in the Wind, 1979

The landscape and its inhabitants are seen very much as a unity in Holdstock's *Mythago Wood*. Indeed the subject of the story is this unity and the unity of our dreams with our environment. Apparently drawing from influences as diverse as *The Golden Bough*, Arthur Machen and modern anthropology, *Mythago Wood* makes powerful use of its materials, reinforming them and proving, as always, that a subject is never dead in the hands of an inspired and original author. It has something in common with Le Guin's *Threshold* (*The Beginning Place* in its US edition), which suggests that the imagined world is somehow connected with the wish-fulfilment or personalities of her young characters (her book is a juvenile), but I can think of no story I have read in recent years which so successfully invokes the mystery and magic of the wildwood. Thematically it has something in common with George Meredith's excellent (and also analytical) poem *The Woods of Westermaine*. If the book's resolution leaves something to be desired, this is doubtless because a second (and final) volume is planned.

Keeton said the words that I knew to be true: "The whole building is a mythago. And yet it means nothing to me . . ."

The lost broch. The ruined place of stone, fascinating to the minds of men who lived below steep thatch, inside structures of wicker and mud. There could be no other explanation.

And indeed, the broch marked the outskirts of an eerie and haunting landscape of such legendary, lost buildings.

The forest felt no different, but as we followed animal paths and natural ridges through the bright undergrowth, so we could see the walls and gardens of these ruined, abandoned structures. We saw an ornately gabled house, its windows empty, its roof half-collapsed. There was a Tudor building of exquisite design, its walls grey-green with mossy growth, its timbers corroded and crumbling. In its garden, statues rose like white marble wraiths, faces peering at us from the tangle of ivy and rose, arms outstretched, fingers pointing.

In one place the wood itself changed subtly, becoming darker, more pungent. The heavy predominance of deciduous trees altered dramatically. Now a sparsely foliaged pine-forest covered the descending slope of the land.

The air felt rarefied, sharp with the odour of the trees. And we came at once upon a tall wooden house, its windows shuttered, its tiled roof bright. A great wolf lay curled in the glade that surrounded it: a bare garden, not grassy but heavy with pine needles, and dry as a bone. The wolf smelled us and rose to its feet, raising its muzzle and emitting a haunting, terrifying cry.

Mythago Wood, 1984

It is the *processes* of imaginative invention which fascinate so many of these newer writers. Yet they have a great deal in common with their predecessors. Where Walpole celebrated "Gothick" ruins, decaying woodlands and antique vistas, in common with so many 18th-century romantics, writers like Harrison and Wolfe maintain their romance with ancient stories by describing an Earth of the distant future. Wolfe, in his relish for the idea of our planet in her senility, has a way of revealing his landscapes piece by piece, of adding one extra element at a time so that eventually you realize how vast or bizarre the scene is. This matter-of-fact method (which has 18th-century models) plus the introduction of unexplained words (most of which also seem to be useful archaicisms rather than neologisms) is what helps lend atmosphere to his stories. Where Harrison leaves things unsaid or unexplained, Wolfe deliberately adds mystery by providing an off-hand description which merely raises more questions.

It seems significant to me that the majority of the writers who have closely followed Tolkien have not produced much in the way of original landscape. Deserts and mountains are vast and forests are dense. In the work of people like Stephen Donaldson (who claims Conrad and James as his masters) they are rarely more than Hollywood movie scenery. Here, Donaldson's hero Thomas Covenant (whose only virtue is his scepticism about the "reality" of the world he inhabits) describes how his world came to be created:

Even to himself, his voice sounded bodiless, as if the dark were speaking for him. He was trying to reach out to her with words, though he could not see her, and had no very clear idea of who she was. His tale was a simple one; but for him its simplicity grew out of long distillation. It made even his dead nerves yearn as if he were moved by an eloquence he did not possess.

In the measureless heavens of the universe, he told her, where life and space were one, and the immortals strode through an ether without limitation, the Creator looked about him, and his heart swelled with the desire to make a new thing to gladden his bright children. Summoning his strength and subtlety, he set about the work which was his exaltation.

First he forged the Arch of Time, so that the world he wished to make would have a place to be. And then within the Arch he formed the Earth. Wielding the greatness of his love and vision as tools, he made the world in all its beauty, so that no eye could behold it without joy. And then upon the Earth he placed all the myriads of its inhabitants — beings to perceive and cherish the beauty which he made. Striving for perfection because it was the nature of creation to desire all things flawless, he made the inhabitants of the Earth capable of creation, and striving, and love for the world.

Then he withdrew his hand and beheld what he had done.

The Wounded Land, 1980

A relish for what is old, ruined, time-worn, is as prevalent in modern epic fantasy as it was in the Gothic of the late 18th century:

But the keep was still quite solid, thick-walled enough so that an earthquake could hardly have brought it down. There were no windows but arrowslits, the tower top was deeply crenellated, and the door was of iron a foot thick, judging by the fact that it had not rusted away in all the intervening years. Time had been kind to the place. Its mortar had grown stronger with age, and only here or there was any stone shattered by frost. It was a redoubt worthy of the name, and it stood there at the center of the cuplike vale with stolid rocky patience, frowning at the surrounding hills, antique and indomitable.

Diane Duane, *The Door into Fire*, 1979

She grew tall and strong in the Mountain wildness, with her mother's slender bones and ivory hair and her father's black, fearless eyes. She cared for the animals, tended the garden, and learned early how to hold a restless animal against its will, how to send an ancient name out of the silence of her mind, to probe into hidden, forgotten places. Ogam, proud of her quickness, built a room for her with a great dome of crystal, thin as glass, hard as stone, where she could sit beneath the colors of the night world and call in peace. He died when she was sixteen, leaving her alone with the beautiful white house, a vast library of heavy, iron-bound books, a collection of animals beyond all dreaming, and the power to hold them.

She read one night not long afterward, in one of his oldest books, of a great white bird with wings that glided like snowy pennants unfurled in the wind, a bird that had carried the only Queen of Eldwold on its back in days long before. She spoke its name softly to herself: Liralen; and, seated on the floor beneath the dome, with the book still open in her lap, she sent a first call forth into the vast Eldwold night for the bird whose name no one had spoken for centuries.

Patricia A. McKillip, *The Forgotten Beasts of Eld*, 1980

Green hills, green wood and a bright river that ran down a gorge to what had been dead sea-bottom but was now — sea. And down on that far sunlit coast he saw the glitter of a white city. Jekkara, bright and strong between the verdant hills and the mighty ocean, that ocean that had not been seen upon Mars for nearly a million years.

Leigh Brackett, *The Sword of Rhiannon*, 1953

And so on. Leigh Brackett's Matt Carse, whose adventures were on Mars, might as easily have been a hero of epic fantasy. He had all the right impulses:

"I have come into the past of Mars. All my life I have studied and dreamed of the past. Now I am in it. Matthew Carse, archaeologist, renegade, looter of tombs."

Leigh Brackett's Mars was, like Ray Bradbury's, heavily influenced by Edgar Rice Burroughs's, but her descriptions of the planet's ancient landscapes were, in my opinion, far more evocative of a sense of magical reality.

This fascination with the antique is combined, of course, with a preference for archaic style. Most of the current attempts at this sort of "high" English are pretty pathetic, reminiscent of children trying to write historical stories by peppering the text with phrases like "shiver me timbers". They borrow largely from Tolkien as usual and produce from his original porridge a gruel increasingly thin and lumpy. Lacking even the schoolmasterly sarcasm and irony of a Chesterton, these imitations are about as valuable, in literary terms, as a faded print of *The Hay Wain*. They are moulded from the basest of metals. They are like mass-produced ikons. They are the literary equivalents of the painted plaster saints and statuettes of Christ found in any Lourdes supermarket, or like those toys produced in their thousands in China and Russia. They are actually made by individuals, but there is virtually no evidence for this. One longs for the crisp, well-written sentences of, say, Mary Stewart:

> From this flowery and winding tract of green the land rises towards the north to rolling moorland, where, under the windy stretches of sky, sudden blue lakes wink in the sun. In winter it is a bleak country, where wolves and wild men roam the heights, and come sometimes over-close to the houses; but in summer it is a lovely land, with forests full of deer, and fleets of swans sailing the waters. The air over the moors sparkles with bird-song, and the valleys are alive with skimming swallows and the bright flash of kingfishers. And along the edge of the whinstone runs the Great Wall of the Emperor Hadrian, rising and dipping as the rock rises and dips. It commands the country from its long cliff-top, so that from any point of its fold upon fold of blue distance fades away east or westward, till the eye loses the land in the misty edge of the sky.
>
> *The Last Enchantment*, 1979

And yet a matter-of-fact style can also produce some peculiar effects as in Jane Gaskell's work:

After two days of rain the little gullies are no longer gullies but the rocky channels of rushing, gurgling, obstreperous streams.

The little crops are beaten and drenched but they are of grains anciently mountain-bred and are not spoilt. They have obviously suffered more from the desultory ravages made upon them by the army before me. I suppose it was quashed wherever possible; the despoilers might even have been executed; but on the whole I think the Northern army can get away with some living off the country here. Amiability is at such a low ebb between the Northerners and the Southerners that it can scarcely be worsened — and we do, I mean the Northerners do, to some extent hold the whip hand because we know how to un-vacuum vacuums.

The Serpent, 1963

For a far better discussion of the problems of style in epic fantasy, as well as an excellent discussion of the nature of the form, I recommend Ursula K. Le Guin's frequently reprinted essay "From Elfland to Poughkeepsie" (in *The Language of the Night*, 1978) which also appears in a collection of essays on the subject of fantasy by writers most usually identified with fantasy, *Fantasists on Fantasy* edited by Robert H. Boyer and Kenneth J. Zahorski (Avon Books, 1984).

It seems to me that not enough modern practitioners pay sufficient attention to the invention of their own specific landscapes: landscapes which reflect the themes of the stories, amplify or at least complement the moods of the characters, give added texture and apt symbolism to the narratives. There is a great deal of self-indulgence, I believe, amongst those who try to emulate the great writers of fantasy. Too many younger authors fail to realize that quite as much discipline is required to create a good fantasy tale as to make any other kind of good story. Attention to landscape, as a specific means of clarifying, heightening or counterpointing a fantasy story, is frequently ignored completely. "Mighty" deserts and "gloomy" forests make for reading which is as dull as the worst of the decadent romances, the goblin stories of third-rate *Stürm & Drangers* or a bad Gothic tale. Descriptive language does not have to be particularly complex or lyrical to work; but it does have to have clarity and freshness. One of the best of the newer epic fantasy writers, who has used the form successfully to reflect her own feminism without once failing to tell a good story, is Elizabeth A. Lynn, a writer who effectively employs a contemporary style in her tales of high adventure:

The Ismenin house was made of stone. It sat

on a bluff, with its broad back to the river. It was new. The original Ismenin mansion, like the other great houses of the city, had been built of red cypress, that beautiful wood which had the property of silvering as it aged. It was Rath Ismenin, Ron Ismenin's grandfather, who had caused the stone house to be built. In the Council Year Ninety-Three, he and others traveled to Tezera, to discuss the effects of the Ban on commerce. Visiting the high families of Tezera, Rath Ismenin walked through marble halls for the first time. When he returned south, he ordered the Ismenin mansion razed to the earth, and built himself a house of white granite, with architects and masons hired from Tezera, under the shocked gaze of his neighbors.

The Northern Girl, 1980

Another writer who has used contemporary English successfully in his fantasy is Colin Greenland:

Dubilier woke. There was light, though the fire had long since shrunk to a mound of cold ash. It was the moon, pouring in through empty window-frames. He put his blanket over his shoulders and went outside.

The ruins shone silver, white and jet. The

magic rays stripped off the daylight shapes and revealed the skeletal forms of a lunar world. Streets and houses became dry gulleys and grottoes; a sagging wall and a pile of bricks turned back into a ragged outcrop and a scree slope beneath. Stalagmites and craters broke the plane of a ravaged plateau. He saw the ten thousand ghosts who thronged the canyons and lingered on the doorsteps of the caves. Their race was new to him: men and women with protuberant eyes, large hands, large hips. They welcomed him. Among them were a few of a different breed, long-necked, lobeless, emphatically erect, like the portraits of ancestors in the galleries of Thryn. They seemed to be gathering around him, pushing themselves to the front of the crowd. We are the road-makers, they said, but you are the greatest builder of all. Perfection on you, master, they hailed him, their parched voices like the wind in dead trees. Ibne, Aigu. Not me, he said. I'm —

He ran. They didn't follow. He came to the road. How could that be the same thing as the broken one they'd slept on, their first night in the marshes? That was a world away; this was a broad road on the moon. From here it drove straight ahead for miles, then plunged and twisted through the jumbled foothill country, lost to sight. Perhaps it reached the mountains. The moonlight turned brick to rock; rock it sublimated, rendering it pure crystal. Hisper Einou loomed above them all, a flawless diamond. Somewhere on those glassy slopes. He was like a pilgrim in an old romance, sent by his lady to fetch an impossible treasure from the lap of a jealous god.

Daybreak on a Different Mountain, 1984

Greenland is also a writer whose work contains elements of analysis. The subject matter of romance is often the chief thematic material of these stories. Greenland, like Harrison, first made his name as a critic of fantasy and science fiction. It is possible to detect in both writers a certain amount of self-consciousness, absent in most of those who went before them. If this sometimes affects the story-telling, it surely makes for improved writing. Here is Harrison again:

The aristocratic thugs of the High City whistle as they go about their factional games among the derelict observatories and abandoned fortifications at Lowth. Distant or close at hand, these exchanges — short commanding blasts and protracted responses which often end on what you imagine is an interrogative note — form the basis of a complex language, to the echo of which you wake suddenly in the leaden hour before dawn. Go to the window: the street is empty. You may hear running footsteps, or a sigh. In a minute or two the whistles have moved away in the direction of the Tinmarket or the Margarethestrasse. Next day some minor prince is discovered in the gutter with his throat cut, and all you are left with is the impression of secret wars, lethal patience, an intelligent manoeuvring in the dark.

The children of the Quarter pretend to understand these signals. They know the histories of all the most desperate men in the city. In the mornings on their way to the Lycee on Simeonstrasse they examine every exhausted face.

"Viriconium Knights", *Viriconium Nights*, 1985

This collection of stories about Viriconium is the most recent of Harrison's fantasy books. In it he has produced some of his very best work to date. In spite of a tendency to repeat himself ("A Young Man's Journey To Viriconium", for instance, has rather a lot in common with the author's earlier "Egnaro", which appeared in his previous story collection *The Ice Monkey*, 1983), this latest work is that of a prose stylist considerably superior to almost anyone else working within this genre.

Harrison does have a tendency to repeat the effects of authors he greatly admires. His homages to the likes of Colette, T. S. Eliot, H. E. Bates and so on may be discovered in almost everything he has written, but the work is none the worse for that. Most recently, however, his admiration for his own writing tends to produce a sense of *déjà vu* which is perhaps not always intentional and moreover tends to emphasize the streak of misanthropism which runs through a great deal of this kind of fiction. It would be a great shame if such talent came to be spoiled by its author turning too much in on himself.

Whatever minor weaknesses Harrison has, he remains the outstanding fantast of his generation . . .

Deserts spread to the north-east of the city, and in a wide swathe to its south.

They are of all kinds, from peneplains of disintegrating metallic dust — out of which rise at intervals lines of bony incandescent hills — to localised chemical sumps, deep, tarry and corrosive, over whose surfaces glitter small flies with papery wings and perhaps a pair of legs too many. These regions are full of old cities which differ from Vriko only in the completeness of their deterioration. The traveller in them may be baked to death; or, discovered with his eyelids frozen together, leave behind only a journal which ends in the middle of a sentence.

The Metal Salt Marches, Fenlen Island, the Great Brown Waste: the borders of regions as exotic as this are drawn differently on the maps of competing authorities: but they are at least bounded in the conventional sense. Allmans Heath, whose borders can be agreed by everyone, does not seem to be. Neither does it seem satisfactory now to say that while those deserts lie outside the city, Allmans Heath lies within it.

"The Dancer from the Dance", *Viriconium Nights*

Perhaps more thoroughly than any of his contemporaries, Harrison understands the value of landscape to his stories. His precise evocation of crucial images acts together with the narrative's other elements, with his characters, both to intensify and complement the story. Perhaps the fact that Harrison reads very little epic fantasy and looks to the likes of Elizabeth Taylor and Turgenev for models rather than to his immediate peers offers some explanation for his success in this genre. Too frequently one gets the impression that, as with the world of science fiction, most practitioners of epic fantasy read only one another's work, a little bit of Tolkien and, perhaps, rather too much Jean Plaidy.

3

The Heroes and Heroines

My good blade carves the casques of men,
   My tough lance thrusteth sure,
My strength is as the strength of ten,
   Because my heart is pure.
The shattering trumpet shrilleth high,
   The hard brands shiver on the steel,
The splinter'd spear-shafts crack and fly,
   The horse and rider reel:
They reel, they roll in clanging lists,
   And when the tide of combat stands,
Perfume and flowers fall in showers,
   That lightly rain from ladies' hands.
                    Tennyson, *Sir Galahad*

Inspired by Macpherson's spurious Celtic "Ossian" ballads which were to give huge impetus to the whole idea of Celtic Romanticism, inspired by Percy's *Reliques*, by Gothic romances, Scott created a form of historical fiction which has scarcely changed. He gave us all sorts of hesitant heroes and noble villains (as well as more interesting minor characters) and probably did most to promote the Victorian ideal of the "decent chap" in popular fiction. Although in antique costume, his heroes (like Tennyson's) with their stolid nobility, their sense of right and wrong, their honest simplicity, lack only a battered briar and a disreputable Norfolk to be everything the right sort of Englishman should be. For all that Scott at his best, and later Stevenson (fulfilling Scott's early promise), could frequently offer a witty perspective on such characters, it is usually true of imitations that they borrow all the superficial ideas while failing to understand the irony which almost invariably gives a book lasting qualities.

For the most part H. Rider Haggard, Conan Doyle and others continued the "decent chap" tradition in romances set not only in remote historical periods but in remote lands beyond the fringes of the Empire. Allan Quatermain, Haggard's greatest hero, was decent about almost everything except "sham" and "wanton cruelty", even when travelling mystically in Time. Quatermain's death, in the lost land of Zu-Vendi, was recorded in the book which contains his "portrait" and bears his name:

And so, a few minutes before sunset, on the third night after his death, they laid him on the brazen flooring before the altar, and waited for the last ray of the setting sun to fall upon his face. Presently it came, and struck him like a golden arrow, crowning the pale brows with glory, and then the trumpets blew, and the flooring revolved, and all that remained of our beloved friend fell into the furnace below.

We shall never see his like again if we live a hundred years. He was the ablest man, the truest gentleman, the firmest friend, the finest sportsman, and, I believe, the best shot in all Africa.

And so ended the very remarkable and adventurous life of Hunter Quatermain.

Allan Quatermain, 1887

Quatermain, like many others, was effectually revived in still stranger tales like *The Ancient Allan* (1919) and *She and Allan* (1926), and in some ways Allan's life was only just beginning as he was reincarnated under other names by subsequent authors, just as Ayesha (*She*) herself was to become the quintessential heroine – villainess of a thousand lost land adventures.

In this kind of fiction gentlemen heroes were the rule: John Carter (the "gentleman of Virginia"), Tarzan (in his Lord Greystoke persona), Merritt's protagonists — all decent chaps, usually assisted by admiring noble savages. Quatermain had the

Zulu Chief Umslopogaas (himself in line of direct descent from Chingachgook, the Last of the Mohicans); Carter had Tars Tarkas, the green Martian prince. These were all characters who could utter the philosophy which, for reasons of reticence and good breeding, the central characters could not. They were full of simple words of wisdom about the horrors of civilization which they delivered in dignified, sometimes archaic speech. Noble savages to a man.

Hawk-eye was essentially in the same mould as Scott's characters but superficially "wilder" — more evidently alienated and suspicious of the world — and the prototype for almost every Western hero who followed him. He was also an ancestor of Mowgli and Tarzan.

Although Burroughs claimed never to have been influenced by the Mowgli stories (Kipling complained of his imitations) there are too many similarities for this to be absolutely credible. In style, in development, in everything but detail and plot they are alike. Certainly there is also a strong hint of Fenimore Cooper in the fundamentally 19th-century style of Burroughs, but Kipling is always present. The simple language of the primitive used to give weight and dignity to simplified ideas about the Law of the Jungle, the nobility of the beast over Man and so on, also occurs in Jack London and has echoes (the use is very different) in

Wells. *Jungle Tales of Tarzan*, considered by many to include Burroughs's best writing, is without question an imitation of *The Jungle Book*. But Kipling and Burroughs were probably the first writers to make the Noble Savage the central character in their stories (though Mary Shelley's Monster is an ancestor). Previously the savages had always been sidekicks — in Scott, Cooper, Melville, Lew Wallace they are there to castigate the over-sophisticated modern world and to die touching deaths. They take the place of the Fool or Jester whose function was often similar in Shakespeare, Scott (*Ivanhoe* gives us both types), Dumas (*Chicot the Jester* may be the first hero of his kind in historical fiction) and Hugo. It was not until the beginning of the 20th century, however, that the noble savage began regularly to serve as a protagonist rather than as a foil.

When Umslopogaas, no longer dependent on a father figure, learning a new kind of self-respect, ditches Allan Quatermain and becomes Conan it is Quatermain who becomes the wondering sidekick, the gentleman "dude" of the Westerns who, in turn, dies a good and fairly noble death. Chingachgook becomes Burroughs's *Apache Devil* (1933). If Queequeg is Hiawatha in revolt then Chief Sequoya (Bester's *The Computer Connection*, 1975) is Queequeg triumphant.

Mutable history suited the romantic storytellers while it was possible to see the past as delicious and misty, but rigorous scholarship and Edwardian scepticism forced them abroad — to India, Africa, China — or into parallel worlds or Earthlike planets where Scott's carping Doctor Driasdust could be left far behind, where unpalatable imagination-curbing facts simply hadn't occurred —where the Red Man still held sway over North America, or an easily understood mediaeval utopia could be found on Mars, or a great, exotic civilization could exist "before the Flood". Even in the Western the romantic spirit maintained itself, but only because it took on, like the thriller, a patina of realism with Max Brand, Clarence E. Mulford and Zane Grey continuing the spirit of the dime novel while pretending to dispense hard facts (and, as often happens, virtually creating a modern West prepared to go to almost any lengths to support its own Myth). The frankly romantic story became primarily fantastic with Burroughs, Merritt and George Allan England in the pulps and Dunsany, Eddison and Hodgson elsewhere. It was not, in fact, until the great success of *The Lord of the Rings* — almost a modern "Ossian" — that the form again came into its own, with the beginning of the recent revival of interest in Romantic movements in the arts.

Robert E. Howard was never a commercially successful writer in his lifetime. His brash, hasty, careless style did not lend itself even to the classier pulps. Most of his work appeared in the cheapest of them. The best was published in *Weird Tales*. Howard seems to be the first fantast to make a noble savage (or at least a sceptical barbarian) the central character of an epic fantasy. Quatermain was always an interloper, an observer of the worlds he visited. Conan was integral to his ancient "prehistoric" Hyperborea and yet much more "alienated" than Quatermain, aggressively contemptuous of Quatermain's values (though not, however, the fascist of the movies).

If the form of Howard's stories was borrowed at third and fourth hand from Scott and Fenimore Cooper, the supernatural element from Poe and others, the barbarian hero of the Conan stories owed a great deal to Tarzan and other Burroughs primitives. Given to impulsive violent action, sudden rough affection and bouts of melancholy, Conan was a sort of pint-sized King Kong. Conan mistrusted civilization. He was forever at odds with both the respectable world and the occult world; forever detecting plots to seduce him. Looking back over his life, when King of Aquilonia, he was able to feel regret for his old, free existence:

"I saw again the battlefield whereon I was born," said Conan, resting his chin moodily on a massive fist. "I saw myself in a panther-skin loin-clout, throwing my spear at the mountain beasts. I was a mercenary swordsman again, a hetman of the *kosaki* who dwell along the Zaporoska River, a corsair looting the coasts of Kush, a pirate of the Barachan Isle, a chief of the Himelian hillmen. All these things I've been, and of all these things I dreamed; all shapes that have been *I* passed like an endless procession, and their feet beat out a dirge in the sounding dust . . ."

Conan the Conqueror, 1936

This passage also gives us a clue to many of Howard's influences. He did not bother to rationalize or disguise the different lands and cultures of his Hyperborean world. Anachronisms are so many they can begin to form the main appeal of the stories. If Scott could make errors involving a few years or a couple of hundred miles, Howard's hero spanned several thousand years of history and thousands of miles. It is as if Conan is trapped in a movie studio, or a movie library of old clips, shifting from 17th-century Russia, to Rome in the first century B.C., to 19th-century Afghanistan, to the Spanish Main of the 18th-century, to the Court of Lorenzo the Magnificent, all the way back to the Stone Age. This melange of influences was scarcely digested before Howard was, as it were, pouring it back on to the page. It was the personality of Conan — moody, savage, boyish in his loyalties and his treatment of girls — which bound all this stuff together and made the stories somehow credible. If Conan was a projection of Howard's fantasy self, he was a very successfully-realized one and a refreshing change from Lovecraft's self-involved neurotics.

The Conan stories appeared in *Weird Tales* until 1936. With their popularity a variety of writers was encouraged to submit similar stories to the magazine. Catherine L. Moore was probably the best of these. Her female protagonist Jirel of Joiry was an amazon driven to martial and occult practices in order to avenge her wrongs (she had first appeared in *Weird Tales* in 1933). The locale of the stories was a kind of mythical French kingdom, not a million miles from Cabell's Poictesme. The stories had all of Howard's drive, were rather better written and certainly more consistent.

She came out into the torchlight, stumbling with exhaustion, her mouth scarlet from the blood of her bitten lip and her bare greaved legs and bare sword-blade foul with the deaths of those little horrors that swarmed around the cavemouth. From the tangle of red hair her eyes stared out with a bleak, frozen inward look, as of one who had seen nameless things.

That keen, steel-bright beauty which had been hers was as dull and fouled as her sword-blade, and at the look in her eye Father Gervasse shuddered and crossed himself.

Shambleau, 1953

Almost all romantic heroes and heroines are wounded children (including *King Kong* and *Frankenstein*), which is perhaps why so many juvenile fantasies are enjoyed by admirers of Tolkien and Howard. Very few adult central characters exist in pure sword-and-sorcery stories — they are either permanent adolescents, like Conan, actual children like Ged in Ursula Le Guin's *Wizard of Earthsea*, youths like Airar Alvarson in *The Well of the Unicorn*, or quasi-children like the hobbits in *The Lord of the Rings*. Innocent, sensitive, intensely loyal and enthusiastic, given to sudden tantrums and terrors, impressionable, sentimental and sometimes ruthless, these characters rarely show mature human responses to their environment, their fellow creatures or the problems they face. They may often do something noble, self-sacrificing or very brave — *as children* — by facing evil down or telling the truth in spite of danger (Alan Garner's *Elidor*, Susan Cooper's *The Dark is Rising*) and doubtless these are worthwhile lessons to childish intellects (for moral lessons — not always acceptable to me — are still present in most children's fiction of this kind: E. Nesbit, *The Hobbit*, the Narnia books and so on). The pretend-adults like Conan (savages and naïve barbarians often substitute for actual children in popular fiction) might claim adult motives — simple greed, sexual lust, vengeance (if that is an adult motive) — but emotionally they are pre-pubescent. Even the cynical characters are cynics of the order of Vernon-Smythe (the Cad of Grey-friars School) and it is very rare to find any sort of real grown-up in epic fantasy (a case could be made against Cabell or currently Kurt Vonnegut for their relentless universal ironies which often have the distinct echo of the schoolroom cynic).

Partially, of course, it is genre demands which influence an author in his or her choice of character. It is often useful to have a naïf as the wondering centre of the story; partially, however, the form itself displays a rejection of adult responsibility and of any sort of sophisticated humanity. Only when T. H. White shifts the emphasis of his story of *The Once and Future King* to the adult concerns of his characters does the book reveal its tragic core, which can be seen as a description of that very process of translation from idealistic youth to humane maturity as the characters reluctantly face the onset of puberty and the implications of their own actions; satisfying the cruel demands of their faith.

A few years after Howard's death, Fritz Leiber began to write his tales of Fafhrd and the Gray Mouser, beginning with the already mentioned "Adept's Gambit" (which was not published until 1947). Though my guess is that they have their spiritual origins in the films of Douglas Fairbanks (*The Three Musketeers, Robin Hood, The Thief of Baghdad, The Gaucho*) and Curtiz-Flynn talkies like *Robin Hood* and *The Sea Hawk*, as well as books, these are unquestionably the most mature and skilful stories to be written consciously as generic epic fantasy or sword-and-sorcery (Leiber's original phrase for this sort of fiction). They are rogue's tales borrowing a fair amount from James Branch Cabell, something from E. R. Eddison, and something from good historical and occult fiction, but they are written by perhaps the most talented professional fantast in America, one of the few writers of science fiction, for instance, to have any real understanding of language or passionate familiarity with good prose and poetry. Ironist, parodist, satirist, Leiber was consistently ahead of his time in the commercial magazines he contributed to and has a record of his work being "discovered" by a large audience sometimes twenty or thirty years after it first appeared. The Fafhrd and Gray Mouser stories rarely contain a wrong note, are full of ironic metaphor, and, significantly, the Gray Mouser is unquestionably an adult hero (though with adolescent weaknesses), the most original to appear in fantasy fiction. Here are the two described by Leiber in his introduction to *The Swords of Lankhmar* (1968):

Fafhrd and the Mouser are rogues through and through, though each has in him a lot of humanity and at least a diamond chip of the spirit of true adventure. They drink, they feast, they wench, they brawl, they steal, they gamble, and surely they hire out their swords to powers that are only a shade better, if that, than the villains. It strikes me (and something might be made of this) that Fafhrd and the Gray Mouser are almost at the opposite extreme from the heroes of Tolkien. My stuff is at least equally as fantastic as his, but it's an earthier sort of fantasy with a strong seasoning of "black fantasy" — or of black humor, to use the current phrase for something that was once called gallows humor and goes back a long, long way. Though with their vitality, appetites, warm sympathies and imagination, Fafhrd and the Mouser are anything but "sick" heroes.

One of the original motives for conceiving Fafhrd and the Mouser was to have a couple of fantasy heroes closer to true human stature than supermen like Conan and Tarzan and many another. In a way they're a mixture of Cabell and Eddison, if we must look for literary ancestors. Fafhrd and the Mouser have a touch of Jurgen's cynicism and anti-romanticism, but they go on boldly having adventures — one more roll of the dice with destiny and death. While the characters they most parallel in *The Worm Ouroboros* are Corund and Gro, yet I don't think they're touched with evil as those two, rather they're rogues in a decadent world where you have to be a rogue to survive; perhaps, in legendry, Robin Hood comes closest to them, though they're certainly a pair of lone-wolf Robin Hoods. . . .

They are the Robin Hood and Little John of the urban alleys, an Asterix and Obelix with adult temptations. Indeed, the attitude of Goscinny and Uderzo to incompetent wizards and pompous authorities is remarkably similar to Leiber's, only Leiber's satire extends to gods and symbols as well as wizards:

Sitting on his dark-cushioned, modest throne in his low, rambling castle in the heart of the Shadowland, Death shook his pale head and pommeled a little his opalescent temples and slightly pursed his lips, which were the color of violet grapes with the silvery bloom still on, above his slender figure armored in chain mail and his black belt, studded with silver skulls tarnished almost as black, from which hung his irresistible sword.

He was a relatively minor Death, only the Death of the World of Nehwon, but he had his problems. Tenscore flickering or flaring human lives to have their wicks pinched in the next twenty heartbeats. And although the heartbeats of Death resound like a leaden bell far underground and each has a little of eternity in it, yet they do finally pass. Only nineteen left now. And the Lords of Necessity, who outrank Death, still to be satisfied.

"The Sadness of the Executioner", 1973

There is a discipline to Leiber's prose which lifts it beyond comparison with any of his predecessors and were it not that Leiber himself is apparently too modest to produce a large fantastic novel, one from him would surely be the best of its kind. Perhaps that very scepticism which colours the Fafhrd and Gray Mouser stories is what has made him hesitate up to now. These are not the ecstatic, wish-fulfilment fantasies of passionate adolescence, nor are they mere fables of human folly. They are generous-hearted adventure fantasy for grown-ups as surely as Stevenson's later historical novels or Hammett's thrillers were for grown-ups. Popular fiction is sadly short of such talents.

L. Sprague de Camp and Fletcher Pratt, who also appeared in *Unknown* at the same time as Leiber, produced for a time an excellent series of spoof stories featuring Harold Shea, a rather bookish sceptic who was plunged into various fabulous or romantic worlds, usually against his will. De Camp in particular has a deep interest in history and has since written some exceptionally interesting historical novels set in the ancient world. He made it his business in various time-travel stories to debunk popular conceptions about the past. In an early story *Lest Darkness Fall* (1941) he sent his character — a descendant of Twain's Yankee — back to the late Roman Empire, and in many other stories he used this device to show his readers how people really might have lived and thought in the past. Shea had adventures in the worlds of *Kubla Khan*, *The Faerie Queene*, *Orlando Furioso*, and various other literary and mythical lands of the imagination. It is sad that De Camp's latest work in this genre has been as a collaborator in writing various pastiches of the Conan stories. I suspect he has a playful relish for bad writing and little judgement where it is concerned, for in *Conan of the Isles* (1968), a collaboration with Lin Carter, we get passage after passage of this kind:

"Sigurd of Vanaheim, you fat old walrus! By the scarlet bowels of Hell — Sigurd Redbeard!" he roared, rising to clasp the burly seaman in his arms.

"Amra of the *Red Lion!*" cried Sigurd.

"Hush; hold your tongue, you old barrel of whale blubber!" growled Conan. "I've reason to remain nameless for a while."

"Oh," said Sigurd. In a lower voice he continued: "By the breasts of Badb and the claws of Nergal, broil my guts if it don't warm an old seaman's heart to clap eyes on you!"

They hugged each other like angry bears, then drew apart to pummel each other on the shoulders with buffets that would have sent lesser men staggering.

"Sigurd, by Crom! Sit and drink with me, you barnacled old whale!" Conan roared. The other collapsed, wheezing on the bench across from the Cimmerian. He doffed his plumed hat and stretched fat legs with a gusty sigh.

"Taverner!" boomed Conan. "Another cup, and where's that cursed roast?"

"By Mitra's golden sword and Wodun's league-long spear, ye haven't changed a mite in thirty years!" said the red-bearded Vanir when they had toasted each other. He dragged one crimson cuff across bristling lips and emitted a mighty belch.

"Haven't I, you lying old rogue?" Conan chuckled. "Why, thirty years ago, when I hit a man in the face like that, I broke his jaw and sometimes his neck as well." He sighed. "But old man Time hunts us all down at the last. You've changed, too, Sigurd; that fat gut was as slim as a topsail yard when last we met. Remember how we were becalmed off the Nameless Isles, with naught to eat but the rats in the hold and what few stinking fish we could dredge out of Manannan's wet lair?"

"Aye, aye," the other chuckled, wiping sentimental tears from his eye. "Oh, damn me guts, of course ye've changed, old Lion!"

This is mindless, silly, heartless stuff which would disgrace even a schoolboy imitator of Conan, let alone one of science fiction's most careful writers. The work is almost certainly Carter's (being pretty typical) but de Camp surely owes it to the Howard he admires to ensure better editing, for Conan was never more dead than he is in these travesties of the original stories.

After his collaboration with Pratt in the '40s, de Camp went on to write a number of epic fantasies that were not spoofs or imitations. Chief of these is *The Tritonian Ring* which borrows certain traditional themes from Greek mythology and whose

hero is Prince Vakar of Lorsk (a nation on the lost
continent Poseidonis). What makes this book
attractive is that, although de Camp is content to
write about a conventional and slightly daft hero,
his control over his material is such that we are
always aware of the hero's defects while remaining
sympathetic to him. We are introduced to him like
this:

> On the king's left sat his younger son Vakar,
> the twin (but not the identical twin) brother of
> Kuros, looking a bit vacuous (for age and
> experience had not yet stamped his features
> with character) and a bit foppish . . . Instead of
> the normal Pusadian kilt he wore the check-
> ered trews of the barbarians, and (another
> fad) copied the barbarian custom of shaving all
> the face but the upper lip.

As well as a supernatural element, this romance
has a picture of the world in transition from Bronze
Age to Iron Age, and its hero, like Airar Alvarson,
has changed somewhat between the book's beginning and its end.

Doubtless reflecting the sober society of the
forties and fifties, which had perhaps seen enough
of corrupted romanticism in the heraldry, rhetoric
and ritual of Nazi Germany (see Norman Spinrad's
spoof on the genre *The Iron Dream*, 1972) the
heroes of this kind of fantasy were much more

down-to-earth and practical fellows, like Jack Vance's Turjan of Miir in *The Dying Earth* (1950):

> ... Did the idiotic visage conceal perception, a will to extinction? As Turjan watched, the white-blue eyes closed, the great head slumped and bumped to the floor of the cage. These limbs relaxed: the creature was dead.
>
> Turjan sighed and left the room. He mounted winding stone stairs and at last came out on the roof of his castle Miir, high above the river Derna. In the west the sun hung close to old earth; ruby shafts, heavy and rich as wine, slanted past the gnarled holes of the archaic forest to lie on the turfed forest floor. The sun sank in accordance with the old ritual; latter-day night fell across the forest, a soft, warm darkness came swiftly, and Turjan stood pondering the death of his latest creature.

Vance's stories remind me of the delicate oriental fantasies of Frank Owen, a neglected *Weird Tales* writer who published a few collections of stories in the thirties, was reprinted in the fifties, but has not, to my knowledge, appeared since.

In 1954 Poul Anderson published what is for me the best story of its kind, *The Broken Sword*. The strong Scandinavian influence is combined with a sophisticated view of Alfheim perhaps owing something to Spenser. His Elf-lords are both more attractive and more sympathetic than his human characters. Unlike most generic fantasy Anderson's story is a true tragedy. A human child is exchanged for a troll-born changeling. Scafloc the human is raised in Faerie, amongst the immortal, sardonic elves. He falls under the power of his own evil sword. Valgard the changeling becomes a bewildered, alienated berserker in the world of men, betraying and killing in his desperate quest for a world where he can feel at home. The tragedy begins to play itself out, inevitably. This superb tale is Anderson's finest dramatic achievement. His later *Three Hearts and Three Lions* (1961), also owing something to *A Connecticut Yankee in King Arthur's Court*, is set in the world of Charlemagnian Romance and again gives us a glimpse of the bitter-sweet world of Faerie.

Anderson has more recently written a number of other books, closely derived from the Icelandic sagas, which do not have the spirit of his first book. Indeed, Anderson revised *The Broken Sword* for its republication in 1971 and introduced an air of uneasy self-consciousness that has lately marked a great deal of his work. For all that, *The Broken Sword* remains my favourite book in the genre and the one from which I derived considerable inspiration for my own early stories.

In my view John Brunner's fantasy, like Anderson's, contains some of his best writing and more resonances than his sf, perhaps because the sf has to rationalize and, to a degree at least, destroy the force of the original vision. Brunner's central character in four novellas is the Traveller in Black, a sardonic, mysterious figure who travels through a universe ruled by magic, battling the forces of Chaos. The book was published in the USA in 1971 as *The Traveller in Black* and has since been reprinted in the UK. Brunner's character was refreshingly unusual, appearing as he did at a time when there were few intelligent protagonists about.

Unfortunately the majority of imitators who came in recent years to fulfil the demands of publishers sensing a commercial market were attracted to what is presumably a compensatory fantasy of homicidal barbarians and grunting rapists. As a result they produced characters even more terrifyingly simple-minded than Conan himself. The appeal was never easy for me to understand, but I was given a clue some years ago when, as a guest of a fantasy convention, I appeared on a panel with a group of sword-and-sorcery writers who told the audience that the reason they wrote such fantasy was because they (and, they implied, the audience) felt inadequate to cope with the complexities of modern life. "Where today," asked one, "can you put an arm hold around a man's throat and slip a knife into him between the third and fourth ribs and get away with it?" The answer was, of course, that the Marines were still looking for recruits. But maybe he meant, "Where can you do that and not have someone retaliate?" If that's the main appeal of such stories it probably explains why most people over the age of eighteen stop reading them.

One other less violently-disposed writer, whose characters were not mindless butchers, was Andre Norton. Although I find her protagonists somewhat too wholesome for my own taste, she has produced a great deal of good quality fantasy which has had a marked influence on the writers who came after her, particularly the women. Norton's sword-wielding riders of dragons and unicorns are young women. This doesn't make her fiction necessarily "feminist" (there's a tendency to claim feminism for any fantasy with a female leading character these days) and it's true that her use of women in what had traditionally been a male role is no more than simple reversal, but they offer a more palatable alternative to Gronk the Berserker. Her heroines are filled with a love of nature and display a caring sentimentality towards the world at large. If her people sometimes are a little too cute (are they trying to apologize for being active?) it's better to suffer that than to be subjected to characters who have the political sophistication of a stormtrooper and the sensitivity of a bad-tempered wolverine. Norton's influence has perhaps been unfortunate, in that sometimes one begins to think the only alternative to Brute is Cute, and one grows sick, these days, of a surfeit of healers, unicorns, nurturers and beast-tamers. One begins to long to come across a female protagonist called, say, Naomi the Castrator. One could tell her to look up John Norman, for a start (but more of that later . . .).

Cute has by no means become the province of women fantasts. Many men, presumably also sickened by the plethora of barbarians, have produced extremely sentimental work. Violence, after all, is only the other side of the sentimental coin, as the behaviour of, for instance, concentration camp commandants frequently testifies.

Another slightly off-beat hero is Stephen Donaldson's Thomas Covenant, leper and minor amputee, who wakes up after a car accident to find himself in a world known as The Land, dominated by evil Lord Foul. In some ways Covenant resembles a character in one of Ron Hubbard's *Unknown* stories (*Slaves of Sleep* or *Typewriter in the Sky*) in that he frequently wonders at his entrapment in a world whose reality is by no means certain. Through six long books (which owe rather more to Tolkien than I find tolerable) Covenant pursues his adventures, though a second, female, protagonist (Linden Avery) adds a certain amount of interest to the final three volumes (which are also, I think, an improvement on the first three):

"No." Her contradiction cut him off, though she did not shout. She had become too clenched and furious for shouting, too extreme to be denied. "He's not you. He's not the one who's going to die." She might have said, I'm the one who kills — The words were plain in every line of her visage. But her passion carried her past that recognition as if she could not bear it in any other way. "Everybody makes mistakes. But all you've done is try to fight for what you love. You have an answer. I don't." The heat of her assertion contained no self-pity. "I haven't had one since this thing started. I don't know the Land the way you do. I haven't got any power. All I've been able to do is follow you around." Her hands rose into fists. "If you're going to die, do something to make it count!"

Then like a quick touch of ice he realized that she had not come here to question him simply because the First desired a destination. *She wants to know where we're going.* Her father had killed himself and blamed her for it; and she had killed her mother with her own hands; and now his, Covenant's, death seemed as certain as the Desecration of the Earth. But those things served only to give her the purpose he had lost. She was wearing her old severity now — the same rigid self-punishment and determination with which she had defied him from the moment of their first meeting. It was the unanswered anger of her grief, and it swept all costs aside in its desire for battle.

White Gold Wielder, 1983

At least Donaldson's characters are adults and are attempting to deal with adult (albeit exaggerated) concerns. The infantile element in epic fantasy still tends to dominate the vast number of books presently being published. This element is perhaps most markedly evident in the work of a writer who originally began a series of books specifically commissioned by Messrs Ballantine to be directly in the tradition of Edgar Rice Burroughs. The early stories of Tarl Cabot, starting with *Tarnsman of Gor*, by John Norman were fairly competent (if somewhat dull) imitations of the Martian books. Soon, however, they became increasingly — now almost wholly — obsessed with a crude form of sado-masochism which, while it is as far removed from *The Story of O* as *I, The Jury* is from *The Lady in the Lake*, was quite as pernicious.

Marked by a droning, obsessive tone, common to much neurotic fantasy, the current Gor books go further than any other books of their kind towards reflecting the aggressive terror of adulthood, sexuality and women in particular, common to so many of them.

Tarl Cabot, who began life as a descendant of John Carter, who was himself a descendant of Allan Quatermain, has a relish for sham and wanton cruelty far more ludicrous, in context, than Quatermain's somewhat pompous chivalry (though both, again, can be seen as sides of the same coin):

Whereas fear inhibits sexual performance in a male, rendering it impossible, because neutralizing aggression, essential to male power, fear in a woman, some fear, not terror, can, interestingly, improve her responsiveness, perhaps by facilitating her abject submission, which can then lead to multiple orgasms. This is another reason, incidentally, why Goreans favor the enslavement of desirable women; the slave girl knows that she must please her master, and that she will be punished, and perhaps harshly, if she does not; this makes her not only desperate to please the brute who fondles her, but also produces in her a genuine fear of him; this fear on her part enhances her receptivity and responsiveness; also, of course, since fear stimulates aggression, which is intimately connected with male sexuality, her fear, which she is unable to help, to her master's amusement, deepens and augments the very predation in which she finds herself as quarry; and if she should not be afraid, it is no great matter; any woman, if the master wishes, can be taught fear.

Marauders of Gor, Book 9 of the series, 1975

Although laughable (and totally out of place in an epic fantasy tale!) this stuff is read primarily by adolescent boys who might be as frightened sexually as the author seems to be. They must frequently feel they are learning what real life is all about. As the blood-and-thunder hacks pretend they are writing of the harsh facts of life and death, so do pornographers pretend they are writing realistically about sex, dignifying themselves as being victimized for telling the truth. I find such writers feeble-minded at best.

At worst they are frighteningly dangerous — for this is, like much present-day fiction, so unimaginative, so seedy in its brutal attitudes towards human beings (especially women), so aggressively sterile, so hypocritical and ambiguous in its moral and social values, that one can only mourn for the tree which was cut down to make the paper on which it was printed.

I am astonished that so many bookshops — especially the chains which exert a certain amount of discrimination in the kind of books they elect to sell — allow themselves to stock such stuff when they frequently show reluctance to take titles of a far less unpleasant character. Since teenagers make up the main market for these books and since most other media have devised a code suggesting what they determine to be suitable for children, one would think that booksellers would be equally happy to exercise their moral judgement. Could it still be that while descriptions of sexual love between adults are thought to be corrupting, scenes of violence towards women, indeed tracts *inciting* violence towards women, are thought to be harmless?

It is a relief to mention an excellent writer, one of the newer generation, Robin McKinley, whose central character Angharad ("Harry") Crewe is a personable young woman who is able to bring just the right note of perfect credibility to a tale of wonder:

Then she found that she remembered her parents together again; as if her mother had died recently, or her father five years ago — or as if the difference, which had seemed so important, no longer mattered. She didn't dream of honeysuckle and lilac. She remembered them with affection, but she looked across the swirled sand and small obstinate clumps of brush and was content with where she was. A small voice whispered to her that she didn't even want to go Home again. She wanted to cross the desert and climb into the mountains in the east, the mountains no Homelander had ever climbed.

The Blue Sword, 1982

McKinley is representative, in my view, of the best of the modern fantasts. There is nothing cute or apologetic about her characters, neither are they brutal, mindless or cruel. This is true of many others, including Patricia McKillip:

She unlocked the gates, her fingers shaking in an anger that roused through her like a clean mountain wind. She snapped private calls into the dream-drugged minds about her, and, like pieces of dreams themselves, the animals moved toward her.

The Forgotten Beasts of Eld, 1980

With the exception of Wolfe and Harrison, most of the interesting fantasy at present seems to be coming from women. Joan Vinge, Lisa Goldstein, Elizabeth A. Lynn, Katherine Kurtz and a number of others have all done good and original work. Since the epic fantasy form has always tended to put rather more accent on personalities and relationships than, say, science fiction, it's an ideal form for good women writers to turn to their own uses. I would like to see a few more fantasies like Joanna Russ's *The Female Man* (1975), making genuinely original use of the genre. There's still a disappointing amount of simple role reversal, of strong, paternal background figures "helping" the heroine in her adventures, of leggy teenagers getting enthusiastic about being allowed to ride a lot of horses. One of the great cross-influences brought by a number of women writers who have chosen to write fantasy is that of the historical romance. Jean Plaidy, Norah Lofts and, on a somewhat different plane, Mary Renault seem to have spawned more than a few imitators who, rather than do the historical research, have chosen to set their timeless love-stories in fairy-tale lands even further divorced from reality than the worlds of Georgette Heyer and Baroness Orczy. These are by no means, I suppose, as pernicious as the male equivalent (i.e. John Norman), but they are almost as bad in some ways because they so often present conventional stereotypical images of male and female relationships, continuing to show men as "masterful" and women as fundamentally passive. Rambofiction makes much the same statements.

Whether their authors realize it or not, they are involved in mass-production. Instead of carving their dolls at a factory bench, they are doing piece-work at home.

While it is very easy to grow tired of the chatty or intimate style in which a lot of generic fantasy is now written it is sometimes almost impossible to get to grips with the excessively distanced narratives typical of Morris or Dunsany. Sometimes such a writer will give that kind of narrative greater dimension by the use of the first person, but more often the writer will merge his characters so thoroughly into the landscape that they will cease to be heroes, in any real sense, at all. Something of this tendency could be found in M. John Harrison's early fantasy.

While he had a relish for his characters, they were sometimes described in entirely visual terms, which gave us difficulty in sensing them as individuals. Also he was inclined to prefer groups of heroes, as Eddison sometimes did, rather than a single central character, so that in *The Pastel City* (1971) we have a selection of heroes but no real protagonist. The nearest thing to a hero is introduced in Chapter One:

> tegeus-Cromis, sometime soldier and sophis-
> ticate of Viriconium, the Pastel City, who
> now dwelt quite alone in a tower by the sea

and imagined himself a better poet than a swordsman, stood at early morning on the sand-dunes that lay between his tall home and the grey line of the surf. Like swift and tattered scraps of rag, black gulls sped and fought over his downcast head. It was a catastrophe that had driven him from his tower, something that he had witnessed from its topmost room during the night.

This tendency is one Harrison shares with the late Thomas Burnett Swann, who began publishing in the fifties with stories set in the fabulous ancient world where Greek and Roman deities still flourished, though their time was almost done. Writing in the first person Swann sustained his narrative adequately:

Where is the bird of fire? In the tall green flame of the cypress, I see his shadow, flickering with the swallows. In the city that crowds the Palatine, where Fauns walk with men and wolves are fed in the temples, I hear the rush of his wings. But that is his shadow and sound. The bird himself is gone. Always his wings beat just beyond my hands, and the wind possesses his cry. Where is the bird of fire? Look up, he burns in the sky, with Saturn and the Golden Age. I will go to find him.

"Where is the Bird of Fire?", 1970

Usually Swann's heroes are pre-pubescent or adolescent boys and girls. Here is the opening of "Vashti", reprinted in the same volume as the title story above:

His mind and memories were those of a young man, but his face and body belonged to a child of six. He was small and smooth and as bright as the sunbirds which clicker like will-o'-the wisps through the forests of the Black Continent. His eyes were the green of young acorns, his lips were the red of poppy buds, and his hair seemed woven of honey strained from a comb and spun into supple strands. Noble ladies liked to caress and fondle him and feed him sugared dates, but when he began to recite the songs of Sappho or the theorems of Pythagoras, they dropped their hands and muttered incantations as if he were an evil-working Jinn. His name was Ianiskos, the "Little Healer". At least, that was the name which the Greeks had given him before he came to Persia to serve in the court of Xerxes, the king.

Swann, for all his predilections, could still draw primitives who were neither naïve nor emotionally coarse and in this he shares something with the greatest and most neglected of historical novelists, Henry Treece, whose novels of Celtic

Britain are the finest I have ever read. There could be a whole book on Arthurian fiction which would include Malory, Tennyson, Swinburne, Morris, Twain, Pyle, Steinbeck and White, and might extend, perhaps, into Celtic historical fiction in general. I would guess that Frazer's *Golden Bough* is a fairly recent central influence. Of all the talented exponents of this sort of fiction — Sutcliff, Garner, Cooper — Treece is the best. *The Golden Strangers*, *The Dark Island* and *The Great Captains* (about Arthur) are models of their kind and superior to Treece's later work (*Red Queen, White Queen, Electra, The Green Man* etc.) which have been more often reprinted. Treece's savages and barbarians are neither noble nor brutish, childish nor sadistic, but living individuals, interpreting their world in mystical and sometimes cruel terms. There are no true supernatural elements in Treece's books, but there is a greater sense of the supernatural than in almost all epic fantasy ever written. To his heroes the landscapes that surround them are full of significance, of hope and terror. Most recently published by the unfortunate and idealistic Savoy Books, it is high time the novels were put back into print.

Keith Roberts, author of *Pavane*, an alternative world fantasy of considerable power, and *The Boat of Fate*, an impressive historical novel, has written a good deal in this *Golden Bough* vein and his introspective barbarian heroes are often the equal of Treece's. Here is a passage from *The Chalk Giants* (1974), a book which appeared in the USA in a badly mutilated edition:

> He flexed his hands, stammering in his eagerness. "This was my dream," he said. "That I *was* the grain, and earth, and creeping things upon it. And mist and sky, the stones the Giants placed between the hills. I was the land, Miri, and the land was me. In the dream I found a woman, who was also the land; and we made children who would . . . know the land, and live out golden times. And . . . this too was the dream. That we died, returning to earth; but we *were* our children, and their children's children, and the golden grain again. It seemed a . . . mystery, a worthy thing."

This is a world after a great disaster, where men repeat their myths and their history according to archetypal, unconscious urgings and tell tales of the past:

> "In the old times," it said, "the Giants came. Elwin Mydroylin was King in the West. The warboats came, the boats of floating iron. Forests grew on their decks. Others sailed beneath the water, hurling javelins that scorched the earth. The crops were withered,

and trees in the passes next the sea. The cities of the Giants were destroyed. Elwin Mydroylin went down to night, and his sons who killed the Dragon on Brondin Mere. He saw the love of women, and it was false. He saw the love of men, and it was false. The Dragons came in the north. The hills were shaken."

Compare this to the flaccid sentimentalism of most of the current crop of "Celtic" writers, the halting simplification of language which lacks all the strength of that which it seeks to imitate, like Evangeline Walton's re-telling of the *Mabinogion*:

He woke suddenly, as if a bell had been rung in his ear. Startled, he peered round him, but saw only sight-swallowing blackness that soon thinned to a darkness full of things yet darker. Of half-shaped, constantly reshaping some-things such as always haunt the lightless depths of night, and make it seem mysterious and terrible. He saw nothing that meant anything, and if he had heard anything he did not hear it again.

Then, sharp as an order, came memory: *"You have come to hunt in Glen Cuch, so why not get to it?"*

"By the God my people swear by, I will do that!" said Pwyll, and he jumped out of bed.

Prince of Annwyn, 1974

Books of this kind have heroes as limp as their prose, but seem to pass for literature amongst a certain kind of half-educated readership. There is a small industry in it, these days. It is written by people busily turning it into a genre as far removed from its roots as the "Gothic romance" or love-story is removed from *Jane Eyre*. It is romanticism corrupted to sentimentalism. Finn Mac Coul takes tea in middle-class drawing rooms and has the refined sensitivity of a Victorian curate; the land-scapes of wild, old Ireland become the well-kept back-gardens of the suburbs.

Macpherson has a lot to answer for.

Happily, there are still writers who can evoke a sense of ancient Britain in their work. Gillian Bradshaw's hero, what's more, begins life as a pretty poor specimen:

When my father received the news of the Pen-dragon's death, I was playing boats by the sea.

I was then eleven years old, and as poor a warrior as any boy in my father's realm of the Innsi Erc, the Orcades Islands. Since I also was a very poor hunter, I had little in common with the other boys, the sons of the noble clans of our island, with whom I lived and trained in the Boys' House; and I had still less in common with my elder brother, Agravain, who led the others in making my life difficult;

almost as difficult as my father's plans for me did. To escape from the insistent world of warriors and warriors-to-be, I went sometimes to my younger brother, but more often to a secret place I had by the sea.

Hawk of May, 1981

While here is Holdstock:

And at that moment I realised that the piping had stopped, and Guiwenneth too had stopped, a few paces away from me. She stared around her, at the flickering lights in the darkness. A moment later she looked back at me, her face pale, her eyes wide, her mouth open; from being delighted, she suddenly was terrified. She took a step towards me, my name on her lips, and I was caught in her sudden panic, and reached for her. . . .

There was a strange sound, like wind, like a hoarse, tuneless whistle, and then the sound of a thump and Keeton's gasping cry. I glanced at him and he was stepping rapidly backwards, arched back, clutching at his chest, his eyes screwed tight shut with pain. A moment later he fell to the ground, arms outstretched. Three feet of wood shaft jutted from his body. "Guin!" I screamed, tearing my gaze from Keeton. And then all around us the woodland burst into brilliant fire, the trunks catching, the branches, the leaves, so that the garden was surrounded by a great, roaring wall of flame. Two dark human shapes came bursting through that fire, light glinting on metal armour and the short-bladed weapons held in their hands. For a moment they hesitated, staring at us; one had the golden mask of a hawk, its eyes mere slits, the ears rising like short horns from the crown. The other wore a dull leather helmet, the cheek straps broad. The hawk laughed loudly.

"Oh God no . . . !" I cried, but Guiwenneth screamed at me, "Arm yourself!" as she raced past me to where her own weapons were lodged against the back wall of the house.

Mythago Wood, 1984

One should also mention both Mary Stewart and Rosemary Sutcliff as important influences on much modern fantasy. Both writers have produced excellent cycles of stories based on the Arthurian myth. Here is a taste of Stewart:

Not every king would care to start his reign with the wholesale massacre of children. This is what they whisper of Arthur, even though in other ways he is held up as the type itself of the noble ruler, the protector alike of high and lowly.

The Last Enchantment, 1979

And here is Sutcliff:

Then Arthur took the sword two-handed by its quillions. There was golden writing on the stone, but he did not stop to read it. The sword seemed to thrill under his touch as a harp thrills in response to its master's hand. He felt strange, as though he were on the point of learning some truth that he had forgotten before he was born. The thin winter sunlight was so piercing-bright that he seemed to hear it; a high white music in his blood.

The Sword and the Circle, 1981

Gene Wolfe, whose models seem to go no further back in time than two or three hundred years, has produced one of the most original central characters to appear in epic fantasy. Wolfe's narrator Severian, the Torturer, looks at the world through genuinely unconventional eyes, although he is very much a creature of his own world. His ideas of right and wrong, of good conduct, of decent style and taste are frequently not at all close to our own. His discursive, lively style most frequently resembles Gulliver's or some other early 18th-century adventurer and Wolfe, through him, keeps us interested, whether it be on the subject of hybrid dog-wolves, fairy tales of the far future, the true nature of magic, the morality of friendship, the qualities of a beast which for a short while absorbs the idiosyncrasies of whomever it eats, so that it can speak for a while like its victim and continue to express the desires of that victim. By introducing archaicisms into his story, casually and rarely explained, Wolfe adds to the sense of reality of his account. I think another reason why Wolfe's narrative is superior to most is because he cares more for his people and therefore automatically impresses us with an urgent desire for their well-being, for knowledge of their affairs. Stories sustain themselves best when they have such people in them. Wolfe's Grand Master of the Orders of the Seekers for Truth and Penitence, Severian, is also that rare creature in fantasy, an unreliable narrator. You can never be absolutely sure that he is telling you the truth. He is also never backward in offering his opinions.

I have never encountered men whose language, costume, or customs are foreign without speculating on the nature of the women of their race. There is always a connection, since the two are the growths of a single culture, just as the leaves of a tree, which one sees, and the fruit, which one does not see because it is hidden by the leaves, are the growths of a single organism. But the observer who would venture to predict the appearance and the flavour of the fruit from the outline of a few leafy boughs seen (as it were) from a distance, must know a great deal about leaves and fruit if he is not to make himself ridiculous.

Warlike men may be born of languishing women, or they may have sisters nearly as strong as themselves and more resolute. And so I, walking among crowds, composed largely of these eclectics and the townsmen (who seemed to me not much different from the citizens of Nessus, save that their clothing and their manners were somewhat rougher) found myself speculating on dark-eyed dark-skinned women, women with glossy black hair as thick as the tails of the skewbald mounts of their brothers, women whose faces I imagined as strong yet delicate, women given to ferocious resistance and swift surrender, women who could be won but not bought — if such women exist in this world.

From their arms I travelled in imagination to the places where they might be found, the lonely huts crouched by mountain springs, the hide yurts standing alone in the high pastures. Soon I was as intoxicated with thought of the mountains as I had been once, before Master Paleamon had told me the correct location of Thrax, with the idea of the sea.

The Sword of the Lictor, 1982

All in all, the Gene Wolfe books possess a style, imagination and intelligence which is rare enough in contemporary epic fantasy. Like Harrison's, his is a talent which, I would guess, would excel in whatever form it chose.

Harrison's most recent fantasy stories have given us a selection of characters all of whom are more clearly described and observed than earlier ones. They tend towards grotesque extroversion (which Harrison in a quintessential English way seems to equate with villainy or moral weakness) or brooding introspection. If Wolfe's Severian is a mixture of Manchu mandarin, Roman senator and 18th-century *picaro*, then Harrison's characters seem to emerge more from a late 19th-century *fin-de-siècle* ambience, as, for instance, with Ardwick Crome:

> Every morning he would write for perhaps two hours, first restricting himself to the bed by means of three broad leather straps which his father had given him and by which he fastened himself, at the ankles, the hips, and finally across his chest. The sense of unfair confinement or punishment induced by this, he found, helped him to think.
> "The Luck in the Head", *Viriconium Nights*,
> 1985

Some come from perhaps a slightly earlier

romantic period. This description, of the chief protagonist, might equally have suited Swinburne:

> He was a strange little man to have got the sort of reputation he had. At first sight his clients, who often described themselves later as victims, thought little of him. His wedge-shaped head was topped by a coxcomb of red hair which gave him a permanently shocked expression. His face accentuated this, being pale and bland of feature, except the eyes which were very large and wide. He wore the ordinary clothes of the time, and one steel ring he had been told was valuable. He had few close friends in the city. He came from a family of rural landlords somewhere in the midlands; no-one knew them. (This accident of birth had left him a small income: and entitled him to wear a sword, although he never bothered. He had one somewhere in a cupboard.)
>
> *In Viriconium*, 1982

This is Ashlyme, the artist, whose attempts to communicate with and rescue another painter, Audsley King, constitute the main thread of narrative. There is a mysterious plague upon Viriconium. While many choose to ignore its existence, Ashlyme becomes obsessed with it.

Meanwhile, strange, careless gods manifest themselves in Viriconium and new lords appear as rulers of the city, as eccentric and hard to place as Viriconium herself.

Harrison, whose own early enthusiasms encompassed a great deal of traditional English fantasy, has come a long way from his sources. While the trappings and exotic appeal of the epic fantasy are retained, he has made of the form something altogether idiosyncratic. Harrison's heroes and heroines are, though frequently attractive and sympathetic, almost the same as earlier villains. Scott, with his robust sense of what a gentleman should be, would see only Oriental decadence here. And Harrison has come almost as far as possible from, say, *Amadis of Gaul*. As John J. O'Connor remarks in his excellent *Amadis de Gaule and its influence on Elizabethan Literature* (1970), "The life of a knight in *Amadis de Gaule* is, above all, a life of action, and his virtue is almost always muscular. . . . Since the only way for a knight to achieve virtue and glory in this life is through combat, the twenty-one books of *Amadis* are saturated with fights. In Book VII, for example, there are more than forty of them, and this number does not include encounters with lions, bears, or other nonhuman opponents."

If there are battles in Viriconium they are usually off-stage. If there are fights, they are as a rule seedy brawls in which everyone is hurt and nothing is resolved, while Ashlyme's nonhuman opponents adopt the guise of guffawing hooligans whose chief acts involve the scattering of garbage in the streets at night, and who are puzzled by the idea of anyone wanting to attack them.

In the new books the magical and epic elements are combined with characters who have genuine passions, adult concerns, complex motives. It seems that in the best of these we shall soon no longer be able to discover heroes or heroines but read instead about real people. It will be interesting to see if the form will be able to take the strain!

4

Wit and Humour

Farther, I remember marking the flowers in the
frame of carved oak, and casting my eye on the
pistols which hang beneath, being the fire-arms
with which, in the eventful year of 1746, my
uncle meant to have espoused the cause of
Prince Charles Edward; for, indeed, so little did
he esteem personal safety, in comparison of
steady high-church principle, that he waited
but the news of the Adventurer's reaching
London to hasten to join his standard.

Sir Walter Scott, Introduction, *Peveril of the
Peak*, 1820

Scott's wit redeemed his work and makes it
possible for us to enjoy it today in spite of its long-
windedness, its unlikely plots, its unfashionable
sentiment. His humorous characters relieve the
sober heart-searchings of his main characters.
Scott, inheriting the style of the great 18th-century
novelists, could hardly fail to supply that wit,
though he frequently spread it as thinly as he

spread the rest of his talents.

Fantastic fiction is happily very rich in comedy, from Thomas Love Peacock to Mervyn Peake. Comedy demands paradox — the juxtaposition of disparate images and elements — just as fantasy does. The square peg was never more delightful than when trying to fit itself into the round hole of a de Camp and Pratt fantasy. Comedy — like fantasy — is often at its best when making the greatest possible exaggerations — whereas tragedy usually becomes bathetic when it exaggerates. Obviously there is a vast difference between, say, Lewis Carroll and Richard Garnett but the thing that all writers of comedy have in common is a fascination with grotesque and unlikely juxtapositions of images, characters and events: the core of most humour, from Hal Roach to Nabokov. Somehow, too, the attraction to wholehearted mythological subject matter is often coupled to a comic talent as in the work of Mark Twain and James Branch Cabell. With *A Connecticut Yankee in King Arthur's Court*, Twain produced one of the greatest classics of its kind, which has influenced more than one generation of fantasy writers. What gives Twain's romance a power which its imitators have in the main lacked is the undercurrent of pathos and tragedy running through the whole story. It is a substantial and enduring book because, although it is funny, it does not deny the facts and implications of its subject matter. The death of England's chivalry before The Boss's electric fences and gatlings is all the more poignant for the comedy which precedes the scene.

Jokes are not Comedy and stories which contain jokes are not comic stories. The art of ironic comedy is the highest art of all in fiction and drama but it is by no means the most popular art. James Branch Cabell's success with *Jurgen* (1919) was based on the public's mistaken idea that the book was filthy. It introduced enough people to Cabell's work, however, to give him a reasonably large audience through his lifetime. His books today are rarely reprinted, as Peacock's are rarely reprinted, perhaps because they are an acquired taste (like some Meredith novels) and no publisher seems prepared to publish sufficient of them to help anyone acquire that taste. A vicious circle. Here is an example of Cabell:

Thus it was that, upon the back of the elderly and quite tame dragon, Miramon returned to his earlier pursuits and to the practice of what he — in his striking way of putting things, — described as art for art's sake. The episode of Manuel had been, in the lower field of merely utilitarian art, amusing enough. That stupid, tall, quiet posturer, when he set out to redeem Poictesme, had needed just the mere bit of elementary magic which Miramon had performed for him, to establish Manuel among the great ones of the earth. Miramon had, in consequence, sent a few obsolete gods to drive the Northmen out of Poictesme, while Manuel waited upon the sands north of Manneville and diverted his leisure by contemplatively spitting into the sea. Thereafter Manuel had held the land to the admiration of everybody but more particularly of Miramon, — who did not at all agree with Anavalt of Fomor in his estimation of Dom Manuel's mental gifts.

The Silver Stallion, 1926

It seems always to have been true that the more grandiose, the more portentous, the less concise, the less truthful, the more humourless a writer is, the more successful he is; at least in his lifetime.

I think my own dislike of J. R. R. Tolkien lies primarily in the fact that in all those hundreds of pages, full of high ideals, sinister evil and noble deeds, there is scarcely a hint of irony anywhere. Its tone is one of relentless nursery room sobriety — "Once upon a time," began nanny gravely, for the telling of stories was a serious matter, "there were a lot of furry little people who lived happily in the most beautiful, gentlest countryside you could possibly imagine, and then one day they learned that Wicked Outsiders were threatening this peace. . . ."

There are, of course, some whimsical jokes in Tolkien, some "universal ironies", but these only serve to exaggerate the paucity of genuine imaginative invention. The jokes are not there to point to the truth, but to reject it. The collapse down the centuries of the great myths into whimsical nursery tales is mirrored in recent fiction: we have gone from hobbits, to seagulls, to rabbits and a whole host of other assorted talking vermin in a few short years and reached the ridiculous stage where there is often more substance to the children's books of writers like Garner, Garfield, Le Guin, Aitken and Cooper than there is in those fantasies apparently produced for adults! That such nostalgic pre-pubescent yearnings should find a large audience in England is bad enough, but that they should have international appeal is positively terrifying. To find them flourishing in the land of Twain, Mencken and Damon Runyon is deeply distressing. But one should not be naïve. America has her own brand of such stuff and much of it is to be found in her modern science fiction.

There is a specific method employed by bad writers to avoid the implications of their subject matter, to reduce the tensions, to minimize the importance of themes which they might, in pretending to write a serious book, inadvertently touch upon. This is the joke which specifically indicates to the reader that the story is not really "true". I'm reminded of my favourite line from Robert Heinlein's *Farnham's Freehold* where the daughter of the family, undergoing painful and primitive child-birth, pauses in her efforts to speak to her father. "Sorry about the sound-effects, daddy," she remarks with stoic cheer.

The laboured irony, as it were, of the pulp hero or heroine, this deadly levity in the face of genuine experience, which serves not to point up the dramatic effect of the narrative, but to reduce it — and to make the experience described comfortingly "unreal" — is the trick of the worst kind of escapist author who pretends to be writing about fundamental truths and is in fact telling fundamental lies. An author of this kind cannot bear to confront reality for a second and will find any means of ignoring facts. Such wounded souls would be joking about the weather in Florida while they burned in Hell. . . .

The great gaudy war-horses of heroic fantasy may look very fine in their silks, their cloth-of-gold, their silver, their iron, their richly decorated leather; they may roll their eyes and flare their nostrils and their huge hooves may dance proudly, but they are inclined to shy at the first hint of cannon-fire, to run, clanking and creaking, at the whistle of shot, to whinny in terror at the sight of blood, and return to the safety of their high-fenced field to make somewhat nervous jokes about the real issues not being decided in the mud and filth of the battle — but on some higher, cosmic plane.

What genuine humour can do, as in the work of Tolkien's contemporary, Mervyn Peake, is to emphasize the implications of its subject matter, to humanize its characters, clarify its issues and intensify its narrative. Humour is intrinsic to the *Gormenghast* trilogy (1945–59). Sonorous though much of the writing is, it is constantly saved from bathos by its wit, its shifts into dark comedy; melodramatic though many of the scenes can be, they are offset by visual ironies, by comic juxtaposition, by sardonic descriptions, as with the Bright Carvers and their annual offerings (something BBC radio failed to understand when it produced its 1985 version). The injustices existing in Peake's world are injustices familiar to us all — cynicism; unfeeling self-involvement on the part of the powerful; confusion and fear on the part of the weak; unthinking brutality and inequalities, frustration and misery — yet these things are never harped upon; more often than not they are laughed at — while the author bides his time.

There are genuine comic grotesques in Peake — the Prunesquallors, the Teachers, Swelter, Barquentine, the sisters Cora and Clarice — the Earl and the Countess of Groan themselves. Even the central character of the first two novels, the infamous Steerpike, is made to behave somewhat ridiculously on occasions, and when he takes his revenge on innocence — on those at whom we have laughed in earlier chapters — their plight is all the harder to endure; the pathos and misery of their situation is amplified and we see their fate in an altogether changed light. This is what the genuine comic writer can do, time after time. He or she can make us laugh only to pause with shock at the recognition of what we are actually laughing at: misery, despair, loneliness, humiliation, the fact of death.

Here is a short passage from the under-rated third volume, *Titus Alone* (1959) where Titus has been arrested and is being tried for vagrancy:

The Magistrate leaned forward on his elbows and rested his long, bony chin upon the knuckles of his interlocked fingers.

"This is the fourth time that I have had you before me at the bar, and as far as I can judge, the whole thing has been a waste of time to the Court and nothing but a nuisance to myself. Your answers, when they have been forthcoming, have been either idiotic, nebulous, or fantastic. This cannot be allowed to go on. Your youth is no excuse. Do you like stamps?"

"Stamps, your Worship?"

"Do you collect them?"

"No."

"A pity. I have a rare collection rotting daily. Now listen to me. You have already spent a week in prison — but it is not your vagrancy that troubles me. That is straightforward, though culpable. It is that you are rootless and obtuse. It seems you have some knowledge hidden from us. Your ways are curious, your terms are meaningless. I will ask you once again. What is this Gormenghast? What does it mean?"

Titus turned his face to the Bench. If ever there was a man to be trusted, his Worship was that man.

Ancient, wrinkled, like a tortoise, but with eyes as candid as grey glass.

But Titus made no answer, only brushing his forehead with the sleeve of his coat.

"Have you heard his Worship's question?" said a voice at his side. It was Mr Drugg.

"I do not know," said Titus, "what is meant by such a question. You might just as well ask me what is this hand of mine? What does it mean?" And he raised it in the air with the fingers spread out like a starfish. "Or what is this leg?" And he stood on one foot in the box and shook the other as though it were loose.

"Forgive me, your Worship, I cannot understand."

"It is a *place*, your Worship," said the Clerk of the Court. "The prisoner has insisted that it is a *place*."

"Yes, yes," said the Magistrate. "But where is it? Is it north, south, east, or west, young man? Help *me* to help *you*. I take it you do not want to spend the rest of your life sleeping on the roofs of foreign towns. What is it, boy? What is the matter with you?"

A ray of light slid through a high window of the Courtroom and hit the back of Mr Drugg's short neck as though it were revealing something of mystical significance. Mr Drugg drew back his head and the light moved forward and settled on his ear. Titus watched it as he spoke.

"I would tell you, if I could, sir," he said. "I only know that I have lost my way. It is not that I want to return to my home — I do not; it is that even if I wished to do so I could not. It is not that I have travelled very far; it is that I have lost my bearings, sir."

"Did you run away, young man?"

"I rode away," said Titus.

"From . . . Gormenghast?"

"Yes, your Worship."

"Leaving your mother . . . ?"

"Yes."

"And your father . . . ?"

"No, not my father . . ."

"Ah . . . is he dead, my boy?"

"Yes, your Worship. He was eaten by owls."

The Magistrate raised an eyebrow and began to write upon a piece of paper.

Of all modern fantasts Mervyn Peake was probably the most successful at combining the comic with the epic to produce a trilogy which can be read and re-read for its insights into our own lives, showing our hopes and fears in a light which is often outrageously funny. The trilogy is reminiscent of Meredith's *The Amazing Marriage* (1896) for the skill with which epic, comic, tragic and moral elements are blended together. It stands above all other works of its type; the *Gormenghast* trilogy is the apotheosis of that romantic form which had its crude beginnings with *The Castle of Otranto*, in which the vast, rambling, semi-ruined castle is a symbol of the mind itself.

"The optimist proclaims that we live in the best of all possible worlds," says Cabell, "and the pessimist fears that this is so."

The optimist and the pessimist constantly war within writers of fiction as they give shape to their chosen subject matter. But it should be the subject matter, not the author's wishes, which ultimately speaks for itself. If authors force the material one way or another to achieve a happy or an unhappy ending and thus deny the implications of what they have written they are betraying both the reader and themselves.

While I admire the work of James Branch Cabell ultimately I find his ironies too relentless. He cheats in order to show everything as an example of mere folly. In contrast to Twain, he uses his talents almost always to avoid pain, though he uses them very cleverly. Nothing is important, says Cabell, therefore nothing hurts. One becomes weary, after a while, of dismissive aphorisms. Like Vonnegut, he seems primarily concerned with showing how ridiculous all human activity can be; how pointless is human sorrow; how silly is human ambition; how pathetic are human concern and sentiment. It is anxiety-quelling of a sort which pretends to realism. It tells us that nothing is really worth suffering for to the extent that people are prepared to suffer; and that we debase ourselves by means of our self-deceits, our ridiculous vanities. But in the end this view is as untrue to our experience of life as that of the ponderous writer who insists that all issues are Large Issues, and that all Quests are in the end Rewarded if He Who Makes The Journey is Noble and Virtuous and given to inappropriate sentimentality.

Cabell's kind of fiction may well act as a fine antidote to Tolkien's, but neither in the long run is very satisfying to the demanding reader.

The impulse to write dismissive ironies often emerges in reaction to an overdose of portentous and meretricious sobriety; but one, though pleasanter to read and considerably more palatable to digest, is finally no more enduring than the other.

Melodrama and irony work very well together; the best fantasies contain both elements, which maintain tonal equilibrium — but a work of fantasy must, like all good fiction, be something more than aesthetically pleasing — though God knows I suppose we should be grateful for the little that is merely that. It should have at its source some fundamental concern for human beings, some ambition to show, by means of image, metaphor, elements of allegory, what human life is actually about. As with listening to the music of Mozart, of Ives or Schoenberg, we wish to be entertained, to escape the immediate pressures of the world — but we also wish, when we read, to be informed, to try to understand how we may deal with these problems and how we may respond positively, without cynicism, to the injustices and frustrations which constantly hamper the needs of the spirit.

The messianic fervour amongst the more outlandish supporters of Heinlein or Tolkien shows, well enough, that readers expect more than simple entertainment from their fantastic fictions. I doubt if there are many imaginative writers who have not had at least one letter — possibly hundreds — from readers who believe that a work of fiction has changed their lives, helped them through a difficult time, caused them to re-assess themselves and their society, and so on. To be a victim of one's own messianism is terrible — to become the victim of someone else's is even worse. By introducing elements of comedy into their work writers can maintain perspective for themselves and their readers. Wit is the best enemy of perverted or fanatical romanticism.

Comedy and fantasy are close companions. If fantasy is real life exaggerated, more colourful and, perhaps, simpler; if the extremes of life are represented by giants and fairies, dragons and heroes, then the vicissitudes of life are represented, in farce at least, by a pratfall or a custard pie, an embarrassing misunderstanding, and the losing of one's trousers at a formal function. To offset the grandiose, the pompous elements in fantasy, the writer, like Fritz Leiber, will introduce comedy to "humanize" the characters and thus involve the reader more thoroughly in concern for their fate. The degree of irony one employs can often determine the degree of sentiment one uses and if one does want to touch on matters about which one feels deeply, then it is often better to use a comic context. Feeling no less seriously about something, one is able to face the implications with a steadier eye. Even in heroic fantasy garb it is possible to canter towards the guns and not shy away from the first or even the second cannonade.

Horace Walpole said that life was a comedy to those that think, a tragedy to those that feel. Since it is fair to guess that the majority of us both think and feel it is fair to expect fiction which appeals to both our thoughts and our emotions. When fantasy attempts to understand the real world, tragic subject matter and comic style can often be the best combination. Byron says in *Don Juan*: "And if I laugh at any mortal thing/'Tis that I may not weep."

But writers must entertain before they have any right to try instruction (even if the only attempt is to instruct the reader's sensibility). Writers have a natural reticence to shout at the same volume the same slogans as those people, quite as miserable and angry as themselves, whose protests at such barbarism as modern war take a more direct and political form. An artist cannot be much of a politician, unless it is during their time off.

If one *is* primarily concerned with telling a moral tale in the exaggerated form called "fantasy" then comedy can have a humanizing influence on what might otherwise be merely a portentous or over-distanced epic narrative. It enables, too, an author to cope with an idea on more than one level. If a writer is working in a form where the ironic tone seems largely unsuitable she or he can supply a balance by having a character whose function is to offer an ironic commentary on the protestations and ambitions of the hero. Thus in Leiber Fafhrd is fundamentally gloomy, while the Mouser is fundamentally optimistic. No matter how serious the drama, humour helps humanize the characters. On a simple level, the use of humour is the secret of the success of most popular film-thrillers, from *The Maltese Falcon* to *Jaws*, *The Wind and the Lion* to *The Man Who Would Be A King*, even *Raiders of the Lost Ark*. One thing that can be said for *Star Wars* (dreadful though the script was) is that it may well have banished the tone of Awful Seriousness which seemed to overtake even fairly good directors when faced with the prospect of doing quite an ordinary or minor science fiction subject.

To try to distinguish between different forms of humour here would be as silly as trying to define different kinds of fantasy and science fiction. It ranges from the wit of Meredith to the comedy of Dickens.

From Homer onwards the world's epics and fables have given us comic characters, including, of course, the original Conan, the buffoon, companion of Finn and the Red Branch heroes, yet there are surprisingly few such characters in the vast numbers of recent heroic fantasies claiming the mythological romance as their particular heritage. The fantasy comic strips actually offer a wider selection of humour. I would recommend, for instance, the adventures of *Cerebus the Aardvark*.

That comedy and fantasy may combine to delightful effect (as in *A Midsummer Night's Dream*) was shown by *Unknown* where writers like de Camp and Pratt, Anthony Boucher, Fritz Leiber, Henry Kuttner and many others came into their own. It is probably not a coincidence that the best writers have almost all shown themselves capable of producing marvellous comic stories. A strong sense of comedy or irony in genre writers ensures that their chosen genre, at least in their hands, never becomes stale and over-formalized. Chandler and Hammett introduced sophisticated humour into the thriller without for a moment destroying the dramatic power of their work and gave the detective story a lease of life it retains to this day, as well as improving the overall level of aspiration of writers.

It was from Dando grown very old and ramshackle, that Beliard heard the same story in his childhood, and he was immediately seized by a passionate longing to be nursed by a fairy. His nurse and nursemaids were fairies; his mother, Lady Pervenche, was a fairy of unblemished lineage; he was born into the most distinguished of Elfin courts; he had never seen anything but fairies — and he longed with childish violence to be nursed by a fairy. Now he was grown up, unassuming and short-sighted, but for all that a credit to his upbringing. He had an intermittent ambition to play the flageolet, and used to steal off to the pool of Barenton where he could practise undisturbed.

He was working at the open-pipe octave, where a hoot at the bottom and a squeak at the top are equally hard to avoid, when he heard approaching wings and saw Puck, the old whipper-in of the royal pack of werewolves, and four stout kennel lads carrying buckets, alight by the pool.

Sylvia Townsend Warner, *Beliard*, 1974

One of the few specifically comic series in epic fantasy is Terry Pratchett's, beginning with *The Colour of Magic* (1983) which sets out, very successfully, to lampoon the kind of sword-and-sorcery story derived chiefly from Robert E. Howard. Somewhat in the tradition of Pratt and de

Camp, Pratchett takes a locale similar to one of Howard's or Leiber's, but where Leiber offers delightful irony, Pratchett gives us broad comedy. It is excellent farce — intelligent entertainment. The *Light Fantastic* (1985) is even better, while *Equal Rites* (1987) and *Mort* (1988) are further sequels. Here is a sample:

All the heroes of the Circle Sea passed through the gates of Ankh-Morpork sooner or later. Most of them were from the barbaric tribes nearer the frozen Hub, which had a sort of export trade in heroes. Almost all of them had crude magic swords, whose unsuppressed harmonics on the astral plane played hell with any delicate experiments in applied sorcery for miles around, but Rincewind didn't object to them on that score. He knew himself to be a magical dropout so it didn't bother him that the mere appearance of a hero at the city gates was enough to cause retorts to explode and demons to materialize all through the Magical Quarter. No, what he didn't like about heroes was that they were usually suicidally gloomy when sober and homicidally insane when drunk. There were too many of them, too. Some of the most notable questing grounds near the city were a veritable hubbub in the season. There was talk of organizing a rota.

As well as a fair amount of original invention of his own, Pratchett offers us dragons who can only fly a few feet above the ground, incompetent wizards, leaking grimoires, and Hrun the Barbarian:

Observe Hrun, as he leaps cat-footed across a suspicious tunnel mouth. Even in this violet light his skin gleams coppery. There is much gold about his person, in the form of anklets and wristlets, but otherwise he is naked except for a leopardskin loincloth. He took that in the steaming forests of Howondaland, after killing its owner with his teeth.

In his right hand he carried the magical black sword Kring, which was forged from a thunderbolt and has a soul but suffers no scabbard. Hrun had stolen it only three days before from the impregnable palace of the Archmandrite of B'Ituni, and he was already regretting it. It was beginning to get on his nerves.

"I tell you it went down that last passage on the right," hissed Kring in a voice like the scrape of a blade over stone.

"Be silent!"

"All I said was —"

"Shut up!"

Most recently Tom Holt with *Expecting Some-*

one Taller (1986) and *Who's Afraid of Beowulf?* (1988) has produced some wonderful spoofs as antidotes for the relentless tide of Tolkienoids still filling our bookshops with their sentimental generalities. Irony of Sylvia Townsend Warner's kind, farce like Pratchett's or comedy like Holt's all have their place in epic fantasy and must surely be preferable to the interminable diet of princesses, unicorns, talented teenagers, doom-haunted barbarians and evil sorcerers which threatens to turn the form into a low-level version of Dungeons and Dragons.

It seems to me that if fantasy fiction is to avoid the stultification that has befallen, say, commercial sf, it would do well to recall its strong bonds with comedy.

"To love Comedy," says Meredith, in his great essay *On the Idea of Comedy and the Uses of the Comic Spirit*, "you must know the real world, and know men and women well enough not to expect too much of them, though you may still hope for good." To keep a form vital you must draw your inspiration not from other books in that form but from life itself, from experience, from knowledge of men and women, and, where fantasy fiction is concerned, from an enthusiasm for the epic, the myth, the noble metaphor which speaks to us on a hundred levels. And to make such things speak to their fellows in as many voices as possible, writers must employ comedy to remind their readers that no matter how intense the images, how grand the themes, how awe-inspiring the terrors, one is still writing about reality.

5

Epic Pooh

Why is the *Rings* being widely read today? At a time when perhaps the world was never more in need of authentic experience, this story seems to provide a pattern of it. A businessman in Oxford told me that when tired or out of sorts he went to the *Rings* for restoration. Lewis and various other critics believe that no book is more relevant to the human situation. W. H. Auden says that it "holds up the mirror to the only nature we know, our own." As for myself, I was rereading the *Rings* at the time of Winston Churchill's funeral and I felt a distinct parallel between the two. For a few short hours the trivia which normally absorbs us was suspended and people experienced in common the meaning of leadership, greatness, valor, time redolent of timelessness, and common traits. Men became temporarily human and felt the life within them and about. Their corporate life lived for a little and made possible the sign of renewal after a realisation such as occurs only once or twice in a lifetime.

For a century at least the world has been increasingly demythologized. But such a condition is apparently alien to the real nature of men. Now comes a writer such as John Ronald Revel Tolkien and, as remythologizer, strangely warms our souls.

Clyde S. Kilby: "Meaning in the Lord of the Rings", *Shadows of Imagination*, 1969

I have sometimes wondered how much the advent of steam influenced Victorian ballad poetry and romantic prose. Reading Dunsany, for instance, it often occurs to me that his early stories were all written during train journeys:

> *Up from the platform and onto the train*
> *Got Welleran, Rollory and young Iraine.*
> *Forgetful of sex and income tax*
> *Were Sooranard, Mammolek, Akanax:*
> *And in their dreams Dunsany's lord*
> *Mislaid the communication cord.*

The sort of prose most often identified with "high" fantasy is the prose of the nursery-room. It is a lullaby; it is meant to soothe and console. It is mouth-music. It is frequently enjoyed not for its tensions but for its lack of tensions. It coddles; it makes friends with you; it tells you comforting lies. It is soft:

One day when the sun had come back over the forest, bringing with it the scent of May, and all the streams of the Forest were tinkling happily to find themselves their own pretty shape again, and the little pools lay dreaming of the life they had seen and the big things they had done, and in the warmth and quiet of the Forest the cuckoo was trying over his voice carefully and listening to see if he liked it, and wood-pigeons were complaining gently to themselves in their lazy comfortable way that it was the other fellow's fault, but it didn't matter very much; on such a day as this Christopher Robin whistled in a special way he had, and Owl came flying out of the Hundred Acre Wood to see what was wanted.

Winnie-the-Pooh, 1926

It is the predominant tone of *The Lord of the Rings* and *Watership Down* and it is the main reason why these books, like many similar ones in the past, are successful. It is the tone of Warwick Deeping's *Sorrell and Son*, of John Steinbeck at his worst, or, in a more sophisticated form, James Barrie (*Dear Brutus* etc.) and Charles Morgan; it is sentimental, slightly distanced, often wistful, a trifle retrospective; it contains little wit and much whimsy. The humour is often unconscious be- cause, as with Tolkien,* the authors take words seriously but without pleasure:

The Silmarillion (1977) is, of course, the finest proof of this argument.

One summer's evening an astonishing piece of news reached the *Ivy Bush* and *Green Dragon*. Giants and other portents on the borders of the Shire were forgotten for more important matters; Mr Frodo was selling Bag End, indeed he had already sold it — to the Sackville-Bagginses!

"For a nice bit, too," said some. "At a bargain price," said others, "and that's more likely when Mistress Lobelia's the buyer." (Otho had died some years before, at the ripe but disappointed age of 102.)

Just why Mr Frodo was selling his beautiful hole was even more debatable than the price . . .

The Fellowship of the Ring, 1954

I have been told it is not fair to quote from the earlier parts of *The Lord of the Rings*, that I should look elsewhere to find much better stuff so, opening it entirely at random, I find some improvement in substance and writing, but that tone is still there:

Pippin became drowsy again and paid little attention to Gandalf telling him of the customs of Gondor, and how the Lord of the City had beacons built on the tops of outlying hills along both borders of the great range, and maintained posts at these points where fresh horses were always in readiness to bear his errand-riders to Rohan in the North, or to Belfalas in the South. "It is long since the beacons of the North were lit," he said; "and in the ancient days of Gondor they were not needed, for they had the Seven Stones."

Pippin stirred uneasily.

The Return of the King, 1955

Tolkien does, admittedly, rise above this sort of thing on occasions, in some key scenes, but often such a scene will be ruined by ghastly verse and it is remarkable how frequently he will draw back from the implications of the subject matter. Like Chesterton, and other markedly Christian writers who substituted faith for artistic rigour, he sees the petit bourgeoisie, the honest artisans and peasants, as the bulwark against Chaos. These people are always sentimentalized in such fiction because, traditionally, they are always the last to complain about any deficiencies in the social status quo. They are a type familiar to anyone who ever watched an English film of the thirties and forties, particularly a war-film, where they represented solid good sense opposed to a perverted intellectualism. In many ways *The Lord of the Rings* is, if not exactly anti-romantic, an anti-romance. Tolkien, and his fellow "Inklings" (the dons who met in Lewis's Oxford rooms to read their work in progress to one another), had extraordinarily ambiguous attitudes towards Romance (and just about everything else) which is doubtless why his trilogy has so many confused moments when the tension flags completely. But he could, at his best, produce prose much better than that of his Oxford contemporaries who perhaps lacked his respect for middle-English poetry. He claimed that his work was primarily linguistic in its original conception, that there were no symbols or allegories to be found in it, but his Christian beliefs permeate the book as thoroughly as they do the books of Charles Williams and C. S. Lewis, who felt bound to introduce their religious ideas into everything they wrote.

I suppose I respond so antipathetically to Lewis and Tolkien because I find this sort of consolatory Christianity as distasteful as any other fundamentally misanthropic doctrine. One should perhaps feel some sympathy for the nervousness occasionally revealed beneath their thick layers of stuffy self-satisfaction, typical of the second-rate schoolmaster, but sympathy is hard to sustain in the teeth of their hidden aggression which is so often accompanied by a deep-rooted hypocrisy. Their theories dignify the mood of a disenchanted and thoroughly discredited section of the repressed English middle class too afraid, even as it falls, to make any sort of direct complaint ("They kicked us out of Rhodesia, you know"), least of all to the

Higher Authority, their Anglican God who has evidently failed them.

It was best-selling novelists, like Warwick Deeping, who, after the First World War, adapted the sentimental myths (particularly the myth of Sacrifice) which had made war bearable (and helped ensure that we should be able to bear further wars), providing us with the wretched ethic of passive "decency" and self-sacrifice, by means of which we were able to console ourselves in our moral apathy (even Buchan provided a few of these). Moderation was the rule and it is moderation which ruins Tolkien's fantasy and causes it to fail as a genuine romance. The little hills and woods of that Surrey of the mind, the Shire, are "safe", but the wild landscapes everywhere beyond the Shire are "dangerous". Experience of life itself is dangerous. *The Lord of the Rings* is a pernicious confirmation of the values of a morally bankrupt middle class. Their cowardly, Home Counties habits are primarily responsible for the problems England now faces. *The Lord of the Rings* is much more deep-rooted in its infantilism than a good many of the more obviously juvenile books it influenced. It is Winnie-the-Pooh posing as an epic. If the Shire is a suburban garden, Sauron and his henchmen are that old bourgeois bugaboo, the Mob — mindless football supporters throwing their beer-bottles over the fence — the worst aspects of modern urban society represented as the whole by a fearful, backward-yearning class for whom "good taste" is synonymous with "restraint" (pastel colours, murmured protest) and "civilized" behaviour means "conventional behaviour in all circumstances". This is not to deny that courageous characters are found in *The Lord of the Rings*, or a willingness to fight Evil — but somehow those courageous characters take on the aspect of retired colonels at last driven to write a letter to *The Times* and we are not sure — because Tolkien cannot really bring himself to get close to his proles and their satanic leaders — if Sauron and Co. are quite as evil as we're told. After all, anyone who hates hobbits can't be all bad.

The appeal of the Shire has certain similarities with the appeal of the "Greenwood" which is, unquestionably, rooted in most of us:

> *In summer when the sheves be shene*
> *And leaves be large and long,*
> *It is full merry in fair forest*
> *To hear the fowle's song;*
>
> *To see the deer draw to the dale,*
> *And leave the hilles hee,*
> *And shadow them in levès green,*
> *Under the greenwood tree.*
>
> A Tale of Robin Hood
> (quoted in *Ancient Metrical Tales*, 1829)

There is no happy ending to the Romance of Robin Hood, however, whereas Tolkien, going against the grain of his subject matter, forces one on us — as a matter of policy:

> And lastly there is the oldest and deepest desire, the Great Escape: the Escape from Death. Fairy stories provide many examples and modes of this — which might be called the genuine *escapist*, or (I would say) fugitive spirit. But so do other stories (notably those of scientific inspiration), and so do other studies. . . . But the "consolation" of fairy-tales has another aspect than the imaginative satisfaction of ancient desires. For more important is the Consolation of the Happy Ending.
>
> J. R. R. Tolkien, "On Fairy Stories"

The great epics dignified death, but they did not ignore it, and it is one of the reasons why they are superior to the artificial romances, of which *Lord of the Rings* is merely one of the most recent.

Since the beginnings of the Industrial Revolution, at least, people have been yearning for an ideal rural world they believe to have vanished — yearning for a mythical state of innocence (as Morris did) as heartily as the Israelites yearned for the Garden of Eden. This refusal to face or derive any pleasure from the realities of urban industrial life, this longing to possess, again, the infant's eye view of the countryside, is a fundamental theme in popular English literature. Novels set in the countryside probably always outsell novels set in the city.

If I find this nostalgia for a "vanished" landscape a bit strange it is probably because as I write I can look from my window over twenty miles of superb countryside to the sea and a sparsely populated coast. This county, like many others, has seemingly limitless landscapes of great beauty and variety, unspoiled by excessive tourism or the uglier forms of industry. Elsewhere big cities have certainly destroyed the surrounding countryside but rapid transport now makes it possible for Londoners to spend the time they would have needed to get to Box Hill forty years ago in getting to Northumberland. I think it is simple neophobia which makes people hate the modern world and its changing society; it is xenophobia which makes them unable to imagine what rural beauty might lie beyond the boundaries of their particular Shire. They would rather read R. F. Delderfield and share a miserable complaint or two on the commuter train while planning to take their holidays in Bournemouth, as usual, because they can't afford to go to Spain this year. They don't want rural beauty anyway; they want a sunny day, a pretty view.

Writers like Tolkien take you to the edge of the Abyss and point out the excellent tea-garden at the bottom, showing you the steps carved into the cliff and reminding you to be a bit careful because the hand-rails are a trifle shaky as you go down; they haven't got the approval yet to put a new one in.

I never liked A. A. Milne, even when I was *very* young. There is an element of conspiratorial persuasion in his tone that a suspicious child can detect early in life. Let's all be cosy, it seems to say (children's books are, after all, often written by conservative adults anxious to maintain an unreal attitude to childhood); let's forget about our troubles and go to sleep. At which I would find myself stirring to a sitting position in my little bed and responding with uncivilized bad taste.

According to C. S. Lewis his fantasies for children — his Narnia series of seven books beginning with *The Lion, the Witch and the Wardrobe* and ending with *The Last Battle* — were deliberate works of Christian propaganda. The books are a kind of Religious Tract Society version of the Oz books as written by E. Nesbit; but E. Nesbit would rarely have allowed herself Lewis's awful syntax, full of tacked-on clauses, lame qualifications, vague adjectives and unconscious repetitions; neither would she have written down to children as thoroughly as this childless don who remained a devoutly committed bachelor most of his life. Both

Baum and Nesbit wrote more vigorously and more carefully:

Old Mombi had thought herself very wise to choose the form of a Griffin, for its legs were exceedingly fleet and its strength more enduring than that of other animals. But she had not reckoned on the untiring energy of the Saw-Horse, whose wooden limbs could run for days without slacking their speed. Therefore, after an hour's hard running, the Griffin's breath began to fail, and it panted and gasped painfully, and moved more slowly than before. Then it reached the edge of the desert and began racing across the deep sands. But its tired feet sank far into the sand, and in a few minutes the Griffin fell forward, completely exhausted, and lay still upon the desert waste.

Glinda came up a moment later, riding the still vigorous Saw-Horse; and having unwound a slender golden thread from her girdle the Sorceress threw it over the head of the panting and helpless Griffin, and so destroyed the magical power of Mombi's transformation.

For the animal, with one fierce shudder, disappeared from view, while in its place was discovered the form of the old Witch, glaring savagely at the serene and beautiful face of the Sorceress.

L. Frank Baum, *The Land of Oz*, 1904

Elfrida fired away, and the next moment it was plain that Elfrida's poetry was more potent than Edred's; also that a little bad grammar is a trifle to a mighty Mouldiwarp.

For the walls of Edred's room receded further and further till the children found themselves in a great white hall with avenues of tall pillars stretching in every direction as far as you could see. The hall was crowded with people dressed in costumes of all countries and all ages — Chinamen, Indians, Crusaders in armour, powdered ladies, doubleted gentlemen, Cavaliers in curls, Turks in turbans, Arabs, monks, abbesses, jesters, grandees with ruffs round their necks, and savages with kilts of thatch. Every kind of dress you can think of was there. Only all the dresses were white. It was like a *redoute*, which is a fancy-dress ball where the guests may wear any dress they choose, only the dresses must be of one colour.

The people round the children pushed them gently forward. And then they saw that in the middle of the hall was a throne of silver, spread with a fringed cloth of chequered silver and green, and on it, with the Mouldiwarp standing on one side and the Mouldierwarp on the other, the Mouldiestwarp was seated in state and splendour. He was much larger than either of the other moles, and his fur was as silvery as the feathers of a swan.

E. Nesbit, *Harding's Luck*, 1909

Here is a typical extract from Lewis's first Narnia book, which was superior to some which followed it and is a better-than-average example of Lewis's prose fiction for children or for adults:

It was nearly midday when they found themselves looking down a steep hillside at a castle — a little toy castle it looked from where they stood — which seemed to be all pointed towers. But the Lion was rushing down at such a speed that it grew larger every moment and before they had time even to ask themselves what it was they were already on a level with it. And now it no longer looked like a toy castle but rose frowning in front of them. No face looked over the battlements and the gates were fast shut. And Aslan, not at all slacking his pace, rushed straight as a bullet towards it.

"The Witch's home!" he cried. "Now, children, hold tight."

Next moment the whole world seemed to turn upside down and the children felt as if they had left their insides behind them; for the Lion had gathered himself together for a greater leap than any he had yet made and jumped — or you may call it flying rather than jumping — right over the castle wall. The two girls, breathless but unhurt, found themselves tumbling off his back in the middle of a wide stone courtyard full of statues.

The Lion, the Witch and the Wardrobe, 1950

As a child, I found that these books did not show me the respect I was used to from Nesbit or Richmal Crompton, who also gave me denser, better writing and a wider vocabulary. The Cowardly Lion was a far more attractive character than Aslan and Crompton's William books were notably free from moral lessons. I think I would have enjoyed the work of Alan Garner, Susan Cooper and Ursula Le Guin much more. They display a greater respect for children and considerably more talent as writers. Here is Garner:

But as his head cleared, Colin heard another sound, so beautiful that he never found rest again; the sound of a horn, like the moon on snow, and another answered it from the limits of the sky; and through the Brollachan ran silver lightnings, and he heard hoofs, and voices calling, "We ride! We ride!" and the whole cloud was silver, so that he could not look.

The hoof-beats drew near, and the earth throbbed. Colin opened his eyes. Now the cloud raced over the ground, breaking into separate glories that wisped and sharpened the skeins of starlight, and were horsemen, and at their head was majesty, crowned with antlers, like the sun.

But as they crossed the valley, one of the riders dropped behind, and Colin saw that it was Susan. She lost ground though her speed was no less, and the light that formed her died, and in its place was a smaller, solid figure that halted, forlorn, in the white wake of the riding.

The horsemen climbed from the hillside to the air, growing vast in the sky, and to meet them came nine women, their hair like wind. And away they rode together across the night, over the waves, and beyond the isles, and the Old Magic was free for ever, and the moon was new.

The Moon of Gomrath, 1963

Evidently, Garner is a better writer than Lewis or Tolkien. In the three fantasy novels *The Weirdstone of Brisingamen* (1961), *The Moon of Gomrath* (1963) and *Elidor* (1965) his weakness, in common with similar writers, is his plot structure. In a later, better-structured book, *The Owl Service* (1970), he improved considerably.

This deficiency of structure is by no means evident in Ursula K. Le Guin, Gillian Bradshaw or Susan Cooper. For my taste Susan Cooper has produced the best recent sequence of novels of their type (modern children involved in ancient mystical conflicts). They have much of Masefield's *Box of Delights* magic. Her sequence, *The Dark is Rising*, has some fine moments. The strongest books are the title volume and the final volum, *Silver in the Tree* (1977), while some of the best writing can be found in *The Grey King* (1975):

They were no longer where they had been. They stood somewhere in another time, on the roof of the world. All around them was the open night sky, like a huge black inverted bowl, and in it blazed the stars, thousand upon thousand brilliant prickles of fire. Will heard Bran draw in a quick breath. They stood, looking up. The stars blazed round them. There was no sound anywhere, in all the immensity of space. Will felt a wave of giddiness; it was as if they stood on the last edge of the universe, and if they fell, they would fall out of Time. . . . As he gazed about him, gradually he recognised the strange inversion of reality in which they were held. He and Bran were not standing in a timeless dark night observing the stars in the heavens. It was the other way around. They themselves were observed. Every blazing point in that great depthless hemisphere of stars and suns was focussed upon them, contemplating, considering, judging. For by following the quest for the golden harp, he and Bran were challenging the boundless might of the High Magic of the Universe. They must stand unprotected before it, on their way, and they would be allowed to pass only if they had the right by birth. Under that merciless starlight of infinity any unrightful challenger would be brushed into nothingness as effortlessly as a man might brush an ant from his sleeve.

Ursula K. Le Guin in her trilogy *A Wizard of Earthsea* (1968), *The Tombs of Atuan* (1971) and *The Farthest Shore* (1972) is the only one of these three to set her stories entirely in a wholly invented world. She writes her books for children as conscientiously as she writes for adults (she is a leading and much admired sf author whose work has won many awards). Here is a passage from near the beginning, again with its echoes of Frazer's *Golden Bough*:

On the day the boy was thirteen years old, a

day in the early splendour of autumn while still the bright leaves are on the trees, Ogion returned to the village from his rovings over Gont Mountain, and the ceremony of Passage was held. The witch took from the boy his name Duny, the name his mother had given him as a baby. Nameless and naked he walked into the cold springs of the Ar where it rises among the rocks under the high cliffs. As he entered the water clouds crossed the sun's face and great shadows slid and mingled over the water of the pool about him. He crossed to the far bank, shuddering with cold but walking slow and erect as he should through that icy, living water. As he came to the bank Ogion, waiting, reached out his hand and clasping the boy's arm whispered to him his true name: Ged.

Thus was he given his name by one very wise in the use of power.

A Wizard of Earthsea

Lloyd Alexander is another American writer who has had considerable success with his books set in an invented and decidedly Celtic fantasy world, but for my taste he never quite succeeds in matching the three I have mentioned. He uses more clichés and writes a trifle flaccidly:

The Horned King stood motionless, his arm

upraised. Lightning played about his sword. The giant flamed like a burning tree. The stag horns turned to crimson streaks, the skull mask ran like molten iron. A roar of pain and rage rose from the Antlered King's throat.

With a cry, Taran flung an arm across his face. The ground rumbled and seemed to open beneath him. Then there was nothing.

The Book of Three, 1964

One does become a little tired, too, of Hern the Hunter turning up everywhere. Another legacy from Frazer. Sometimes he appears in books of this kind almost as an embarrassment, as if convention demands his presence: an ageing and rather vague bishop doing his bit at official services.

There are a good many more such fantasies now being written for children and on the whole they are considerably better than the imitations written ostensibly for adults. Perhaps the authors feel more at ease when writing about and for children — as if they are forced to tell fewer lies (or at least answer fewer fundamental questions) to themselves or their audience.

Among these newer writers, Gillian Bradshaw has produced yet another Arthurian trilogy. This one, however, is written from the point of view of Gwalchmai, the son of the King of Orkney and Queen Morgawse (who might be a sorceress). He encounters the Sidhe, some of whom help him as he journeys to be with King Arthur who is fighting a desperate battle against the Saxon invaders. Bradshaw's writing is clear and vibrant, her story-telling has pace and verve.

> She lifted her arms and the Darkness leapt. But she was distant again, and I stood at Camlann. I looked up and saw Lugh standing in the west, opposite Morgawse, holding his arm above the island so that the Queen could not touch it. Behind him was light too brilliant, too glorious to be seen. For a moment I saw these two confronting one another, and then my field of vision narrowed. I saw the island and the figures of armies. I saw the Family and myself in it. The armies began to move, and the sounds of battle arose. I realized that I saw things that were yet to come, and was terrified. I covered my face with my arms and cried, "No more!"
> And abruptly there was silence.
>
> *Hawk of May*, 1981

The subsequent books in this sequence are *Kingdom of Summer* (1982) and *In Winter's Shadow* (1983).

Several of the emerging children's novelists actually display more original gifts and greater talent than the majority of those writing ostensibly for adults. In my view Robin McKinley is one of the very best of these. Her *The Blue Sword* (1982) won the John Newbery Medal in 1984 and she is building an excellent reputation. *The Blue Sword* is the first of her Chronicles of Damar. She has a fresh and interesting approach to the genre which immediately makes it into something of her own. Her style is robust, elegant and considered, qualities which are a great relief after so many clunking archaicisms and cuticisms which inhabit the great majority of present-day fantasies. Angharad Crewe, the young woman who is her central character, is far more likeable than the tribe of leggy, slightly awkward, pony-loving teenagers appearing all too frequently in recent fantasies. Again McKinley's writing makes me wish I had been able to read them when I was young. They would have been a wonderful antidote to The Famous Five and the interminable valleys, mountains, lakes and forests of Adventure which was most of what we were offered after Enid Blyton had become an acceptable brand name on all the myriad planes and demi-planes of the English middle class.

The power that washed over that face, that rolled down the arms and into the sword and shield, was that of demonkind, and Harry knew she was no match for this one, and in spite of the heat of Gonturan in her hand her heart was cold with fear. The two stallions reared again and reached out to tear each other; the white stallion's neck was now ribboned with blood, like the real ribbons he wore in his mane. Harry raised her sword arm and felt the shock of the answer, the hilts of the swords ring together, and sparks flew from the crash, and it seemed that the smoke rose from them and blinded her. The other rider's hot breath was in her face. His lips parted and she saw his tongue: it was scarlet, and looked more like fire than living flesh.

The Blue Sword

After reading a good many of these contemporary fantasy stories I remained impressed by the number of authors of adult books who described their characters as children and the number of children's writers who produce perfectly mature and sensible characters who think and act intelligently. I found myself wishing that the likes of McKinley would choose to do more work for grown-ups. Perhaps the reason they don't is that they find they can, writing for teenagers, preserve a greater respect for their audience.

Another variety of book has begun to appear, a sort of Pooh-fights-back fiction of the kind produced by Richard Adams, which substitutes animals for human protagonists, contains a familiar set of middle-class Christian undertones (all these books seem to be written with a slight lisp) and is certainly already more corrupt than Tolkien. Adams is a worse writer but he must appeal enormously to all those many readers who have never quite lost their yearning for the frisson first felt when Peter Rabbit was expelled from Mr MacGregor's garden:

As Dandelion ended, Acorn, who was on the windward side of the little group, suddenly started and sat back, with ears up and nostrils twitching. The strange, rank smell was stronger than ever and after a few moments they all heard a heavy movement close by. Suddenly, on the other side of the path, the fern parted and there looked out a long, dog-like head, striped black and white. It was pointed downward, the jaws grinning, the muzzle close to the ground. Behind, they could just discern great, powerful paws and a shaggy black body. The eyes were peering at them, full of savage cunning. The head moved slowly, taking in the dusky lengths of the wood ride in both directions, and then fixed them once more with its fierce, terrible stare. The jaws opened wider and they could see the teeth, glimmering white as the stripes along the head. For long moments it gazed and the rabbits remained motionless, staring back without a sound. Then Bigwig, who was nearest to the path, turned and slipped back among the others.

"A lendri," he muttered as he passed through them. "It may be dangerous and it may not, but I'm taking no chances with it. Let's get away."

Watership Down, 1972

Adams's follow-up to this was *Shardik* (1974), better written, apparently for adults, and quite as silly. It was about a big bear who died for our sins: *Martyred Pooh*. Later, *The Plague Dogs* (1977) displayed an almost paranoid conservative misanthropism.

I sometimes think that as Britain declines, dreaming of a sweeter past, entertaining few hopes for a finer future, her middle classes turn increasingly to the fantasy of rural life and talking animals, the safety of the woods that are the pattern of the paper on the nursery-room wall. Hippies, housewives, civil servants, share in this wistful trance; eating nothing as dangerous or exotic as the lotus, but chewing instead on a form of mildly anaesthetic British cabbage. If the bulk of American sf could be said to be written by robots, about robots, for robots, then the bulk of English fantasy seems to be written by rabbits, about rabbits and for rabbits.

How much further can it go?

Of the children's writers only Lewis and Adams are guilty, in my opinion, of producing thoroughly corrupted romanticism — sentimentalized pleas for moderation of aspiration which are at the root of this kind of Christianity. In Lewis's case this consolatory, anxiety-stilling "Why try to play Mozart when it's easier to play Rodgers and Hammerstein?" attitude extended to his non-fiction, particularly the dreadful but influential *Experiment in Criticism*. But these are, anyway, minor figures. It is Tolkien who is most widely read and worshipped. And it was Tolkien who most betrayed the romantic discipline, more so than ever Tennyson could in *Idylls of the King*, which enjoyed a similar vogue in Victorian England.

Corrupted romanticism is as unwholesome as the corrupted realism of, say, Harold Robbins. Cabell's somewhat obvious irony is easier to take than Tolkien's less obvious sentimentality, largely because Cabell's writing is wittier, more inventive and better disciplined. I find William Morris naïve and silly but essentially good-hearted (and a better utopianist than a fantast); Dunsany I find slight but inoffensive. Lewis speaks for the middle-class status quo, as, more subtly, does Charles Williams. Lewis uses the stuff of fantasy to preach sermons quite as nasty as any to be found in Victorian sentimental fiction, and he writes badly. A group of self-congratulatory friends can often ensure that any writing emerging from it remains hasty and unpolished.

Ideally fiction should offer us escape and force us, at least, to ask questions; it should provide a release from anxiety but give us some insight into the causes of anxiety. Lin Carter, in his *Imaginary Worlds* — the only book I have been able to find on the general subject of epic fantasy — uses an argument familiar to those who are used to reading apologies from that kind of sf or thriller buff who feels compelled to justify his philistinism: "The charge of 'escapist reading'," says Carter, "is most often levelled against fantasy and science fiction by those who have forgotten or overlooked the simple fact that virtually all reading — all music and poetry and art and drama and philosophy for that matter — is a temporary escape from what is around us." Like so many of his colleagues in the professional sf world, Carter expresses distaste for fiction which is not predominantly escapist by charging it with being "depressing" or "negative" if it does not provide him with the moral and psychological comforts he seems to need.

Carter dismisses Spenser as "dull" and Joyce as "a titanic bore" and writes in clichés, euphemisms and wretchedly distorted syntax, telling us that the Pre-Raphaelites were "lisping exquisites" and that Ford Madox Brown (1821–93) was a young man attracted to the movement by Morris's (1834–96) fiery Welsh (born Walthamstow, east London) dynamism and that because Tolkien got a CBE (not a knighthood) we must now call him "Sir John" —but Carter, at least, is not the snob some American adherents are (and there is nobody more risible than the provincial American literary snob — Gore Vidal being the most developed example). In a recent anthology compiled by Robert H. Boyer and Kenneth J. Zahorski, *The Fantastic Imagination*, we find the following: "In addition to their all being high fantasy, the stories selected here are good literature." Amongst the writers to be found in the volume are C. S. Lewis, John Buchan, Frank R. Stockton and Lloyd Alexander, not one of whom can match the literary talents of, say, Fritz Leiber, whose work has primarily been published in commercial magazines and genre paperback series. For years American thriller buffs with pretensions ignored Hammett and Chandler in favour of inferior English writers like D. L. Sayers and here we see the same thing occurring with American fantasy writers. The crux of the thing remains: the writers admired are not "literary" or "literate". As often as not they flatter middle-brow sensibilities and reinforce middle-class sentimentality and therefore do not threaten a carefully maintained set of social and intellectual assumptions.

Yet Tennyson inspired better poets who followed him, who sought the origin of his inspiration and made nobler use of it. Both Swinburne and Morris could, for instance, employ the old ballad metres more effectively than Tennyson himself, refusing, unlike him, to modify their toughness. Doubtless Tolkien will also inspire writers who will take his raw materials and put them to nobler uses. I would love to believe that the day of the rural romance is done at last.

6

Excursions and Developments

SELIM: Do you believe in magic, Hassan?

HASSAN: Men who think themselves wise believe nothing till the proof. Men who are wise believe anything till the disproof.

SELIM: What do we know if magic be a lie or not? But, since it is certain that only magic will avail you, you may as well put it to the test.

James Elroy Flecker, *The Story of Hassan of Bagdad and how he came to make the Golden Journey to Samarkand*, 1922

It has always been my belief that category definitions in the arts are destructive both of the thing they try to describe and of the aspiration of the artist. They produce an unnecessary self-consciousness. They are convenient only to substandard academic discussion and cynical commercial exploitation.

"Schools" and "movements" exist, usually for very short periods, because conservative and authoritarian elements force individuals to club together against them. A school prolonged past its immediate necessity for existence becomes, like sf, itself conservative and rigid, producing rivals. Once a movement comes into vogue it is not unusual for its original adherents to reject it and move to more "secret" territory. Artists must constantly reject and then rediscover the past in their search for a vocabulary that is both private and universal; cults, secret languages, enthusiasm for unfashionable, forgotten or "undiscovered" hero-models, displays of dandyism and sensational social and artistic behaviour are all part of the equipment of individuals seeking confidence and assertiveness in a world to which they feel opposed. The impulse was as common to Pre-Raphaelites as to modern rock music enthusiasts. Fashion is our enemy.

"Epic fantasy" is a meaningless term — as meaningless as "science fiction" — but we know roughly what is described by it. It covers a range of fiction from Morris to Peake; it is used for quite opposite intentions, in a wide variety of styles. It can be rarefied or it can be very crude; humane or misanthropic; "escapist" or "serious". Finally, and with the exception of hacks who seek and purvey the lowest common denominators, it is as varied in expression as the temperaments of those who produce it. We have late flower-power styles on the one hand and comic-book-derived styles on the other — they are good or bad according to who uses them.

Essentially they are all expressions of a second Romantic Revival which began to gather force in the late sixties, with drugs and rock music as its most potent and obvious expressions. As with most Romantic movements it has its share of dead heroes — for Keats, Shelley and Byron we can substitute Brian Jones, Jimi Hendrix and Jim Morrison — their work was different but their life-styles, their ambitions, their appeal to the general public as *Romantic characters of their own invention* was similar, and they aroused the same kind of bitter envy in journalists and lesser contemporaries as their predecessors. Perhaps it would be fairer to make comparisons between rock stars and the figures of the Aesthetic movement, like Dowson, Beardsley or even Wilde. The work is wholly different in everything but spirit, of course, but the comparisons are obvious. It is not a coincidence that there has been for some time a definite overlap between this kind of rock music and fantastic literature or art. There are many obvious examples: bands deriving names and titles of songs from Tolkien, Peake and others, in the sixties there were the "psychedelic" and "heavy metal" science-fiction-orientated bands and performers. Survivors into the eighties include Pink Floyd, Hawkwind, Blue Oyster Cult, David Bowie and many others. There have been whole record conceptions like *The King of Elfland's Daughter*. When Rodney Matthews painted the Rolling Stones as worn-out heroes of a sword-and-sorcery story he captured perfectly the important crosscurrents of the new romanticism.

It could be that until recently this romantic drive, in politics and the arts, was confined to a relative minority in the West, but with an increase in population, with a majority of that population being young, we are now witnessing an emphatic shift in artistic and literary taste which is bewildering and frightening to those whose opinions were formed in an earlier social climate.

That these impulses are in one sense "immature" cannot be denied, but uncritical enthusiasm is better than apathy, particularly in the arts, and the cult of the Romantic Hero can only be disturbing if it is translated into violent and simplistic political theory.

Side by side with an atavistic relish for swords and dragons is an appreciation of the new, rich language of modern life, of the singers, like Bruce

Springsteen, who celebrate it in urban romantic images — "Snakeskin suits packed with Detroit muscle . . ." — of punk heroes who could so easily be the Gray Mouser in black plastic jackets and drainpipe jeans. The West has never at any single time possessed such a wealth of romantic imagery and talent, but it has hardly begun to flower; we could be witnessing only the germinal stages, for there has yet to be developed a literary and visual vocabulary to reflect the impact of so much raw material.

The astonishment of writers of epic fantasy who saw their work gaining a wide audience must have been something like the feelings experienced by the old black blues-singers of the late fifties who were brought from obscurity in America to England and the Continent to discover that they were heroes to the large audiences waiting to hear them. Within ten years we have seen books which were originally published in small editions and often remaindered enjoying large sales. Coupled with a revival of fantasy "classics", excellent out-of-print books of genuine merit, like Leiber's and Anderson's, have been reprinted. And side by side with this have been the visual examples as more and more talented artists found a market for their work. From the crude and rather over-rated "Marvel" style, with its emphasis on distorted perspective, purple prose and increasingly unimaginative sensationalism, to the later work of Barry Smith, Howard Chaykin and others, the comics have reflected this new interest.

In the past five years or so there has been a vast number of comic books launched in America, France and England, all dealing with sword-and-sorcery and related fantasy characters. Tarzan has enjoyed a revival. John Carter had his own strip, as had Conan. There have been various spin-offs from the Conan series with other characters like Kull, Solomon Kane and Red Sonja. Fafhrd and the Gray Mouser (drawn by Chaykin, one of the most talented exponents of this kind of visual narrative) have appeared in a number of strip adventures. Barry Smith — the quintessential Conan artist — has his own following who buy his beautifully produced posters. Many of the artists who do strips, posters and book jackets have large fan-followings in their own right — Roger Dean, Frank Frazetta, Jeff Jones, Jim Cawthorn, Corben and many, many more. The small, enthusiast presses who began to emerge a few years ago are, from barely breaking even, now making substantial profits.

In some senses the "Golden Age" of the sixties and seventies, with its proliferation of fantastic posters and full-colour picture books, is over. Some of the firms, like Big O, seemed so thoroughly geared to the optimism and sense of wonder that emerged in the sixties that they rose naturally on the crest of a social wave — and crashed dramatically when it struck the economic rocks of the late seventies and early eighties. But private presses continue to do lavish de-luxe illustrated editions of "fantasy classics" like *The Dying Earth*, *The Tritonian Ring* and *Black God's Kiss*. There are a number of minor industries specializing in Howardiana and Tolkieniana. In Howard's case these high-priced, well-produced books, pamphlets and posters probably make more money for their publishers than Howard ever earned in his entire career.

The success of *Star Wars* meant that more producers and directors became interested in producing unashamedly romantic science fiction and fantasy movies. Few of these have been much good up to now. I find the Conan movies both derivative (of elements which in themselves are derived and debased from Howard's) and silly. They have very rapidly, moreover, degenerated into complete meaninglessness — and the public, it seems, objects. When *Red Sonja* (1985) was released in the U.S. and Britain it was scarcely in the theatres long enough for anyone to see it all the way through. I have deliberately resisted discussing the sword-and-sorcery movies which have emerged since the late seventies. I find them all disappointing, whether they consist of live action or are animated.

The people who make the movies seem to have no genuine love for the form (as Ford had, for instance, for the Western) and this surely is the main thing we understand when watching them. Since the overall standard of entertainment movies is low at present, I suppose this is reflected in the bad quality of the fantasy films. We have entered a decadent period in both the theatre and the cinema, in my view, reminiscent of the 18th century's emphasis on sensation and gory special effects on the stage, with more attention being given to the dramatic "change" than to the written words. We have progressed naturally, it seems, once again from true Romanticism to the infantile nonsense of Grand Guignol.

In the late seventies epic fantasy was, compared to the related sub-genre of science fiction, in its infancy as a commercial form. Even then, however, there were authors prepared to hack out the inevitable imitations to supply exploitative publishers. Such publishers impose strictures on their writers and thus ensure that original works of fantasy are sometimes in danger of being lost in the general slew of trash and not understood by critics who have already begun to react in terms of generic precedents (typically this kind of fantasy is sent to sf reviewers who find it lacking because, they say, it "isn't proper science fiction").

I suppose it will not greatly matter if, out of all this dross, good things emerge. We have seen the likes of Le Guin, Harrison, Wolfe and Russ make something of their own from the form. Each of these writers is very different in character, style and intention, yet they are all extremely talented. Other newer writers, like McKinley, Goldstein, Greenland, Pratchett, McKillip, Powers and Ryman are emerging, also showing signs of moulding the form to their own specific needs. Epic fantasy is much closer to the mainstream of romantic fiction than science fiction which was, itself, largely derived from such fantasy. It is a more flexible form. We have already seen what talented writers can do with sf, so it would stand to reason that the next few years should see some excellent developments.

How much fantasy fiction has influenced "mainstream" writers it is hard to tell. Much of what is published today that is good has close affinities with the work of, say, Harrison or Russ. In turn one can hope that these writers will influence the fantasy genre. We need more writers who will take the generic elements and turn them into something personal, something which has memorable individuals or characters, which bears the mark of an idiosyncratic style, which makes use of language the way, for instance, Robert Nye has done in his pastiche memoirs of Falstaff,

Merlin, Faust and Sir Walter Raleigh, or even employ the range of symbolism and structure for more experimental story-telling, as Peter Ackroyd did recently in *Hawksmoor*, as John Crowley does in such books as *Little, Big* or as Robert Meadley has done in *Return to Ost* (1987), a wonderfully original use of the epic fantasy form, or as Lucius Shepard appears to be doing with sf in stories like *Green Eyes* (1984). I would personally like to see more women writers bringing their ideas and dynamic to the form. It is, after all, a genre which owes as much to the female novelists of the 18th and 19th centuries as it does to the men. Without Mary Shelley, Clara Reeve, Ann Radcliffe and scores of others, the epic fantasy tale could not exist in its present form.

The influence of the South American "fantastic realists" is beginning to show in some of the younger writers' work. In my view a little more of this influence could do no harm. It can be argued that it is a good test of a writer if he or she is able to make existing conventions seem completely fresh. As long as it attracts such writers, a genre never really perishes. It can be pronounced dead only to spring to life again, lusher than ever. Genres are always being rediscovered or re-invented, certainly reinterpreted, and a form with its origins so close to our unconscious, to myth and folklore, will continue to attract talented writers. If I bemoan the fact that most of the stuff published is shallow, imitative, worthless and without genuine resonances, either literary or psychological, it is not to attack what is good, vital, stimulating. It is just that I wish there were a bit more of it about.

One of the peculiar developments in the past ten years or so has been the rise of the "Dungeons and Dragons" industry. These role-playing games are derived directly from epic fantasy. They owe everything to the original writers like Howard or Tolkien. Thousands of people — mostly teenagers — live out large parts of their lives questing for treasures, outwitting wizards and doing in dragons. I must admit that these games are too complex for me and, while they hold no attraction, I am fascinated by the elaborate pains people take in playing them. What is more, people are now frequently buying books because they are curious to discover the origins of their favourite game. This industry has led to writers producing books which are essentially templates for role-playing games. It is a subject I'm not qualified to discuss and I am sure there must be a number of books which deal with the phenomenon itself. The kid you see in the street who appears to be the village idiot might well have a huge IQ. He also happens to "be" Gorijor the Thief, on a dangerous mission to the City of Slithering Salamanders. And that bulge in his pocket could well be a selection of toy models, each one of which is a character in a complicated drama being enacted across a district, sometimes an entire country! Together with the rise of the computer game, the fantasy-role-playing game is having an impact on children which is extremely difficult to gauge. What was virtually a formless ambience in my eleven-year-old head is probably a highly codified and fully understood structure in the head of today's eleven-year-old. The impulses are the same, but there are now huge industries (like those which produce all kinds of movie "spin-offs") ready to tap into them, to exploit them commercially, to supply them with rules. (For once I find myself incapable of drawing a moral lesson from this!)

Commercial interests, of course, are always in the process of "taking away" from the people, formalizing and sanitizing something and selling it back to them, just as commercial interests successfully institutionalized so much rock music and produced bland, superficial, unthreatening copies of the styles of the great originals. If this continues to happen to epic fantasy, we shall probably experience a typical reaction. Publishers will be found with a great deal of rubbish on their hands which nobody wants. At this stage, publishers usually announce that the genre they have bled white "no longer sells". The danger of this is that the public will then be denied access to those good writers who have soldiered on regardless, ignoring the fluctuations of fashion and the commercial demands of a "market" which half the time doesn't have the slightest idea what the public wants or why.

One thing, I think, is certain: this revival of direct and unashamed romanticism will have some sort of lasting effect. Compared to its influence on the popular arts, its influence in literature and painting has been minimal, but it is beginning to show. Ultimately it could have a stronger influence on a new generation than science fiction had on the "pop" painters and novelists who enjoyed their vogue in the fifties and sixties.

For too long now we have experienced the restraints and self-consciousness of a predominantly middle-class, pompously male and cautious literary establishment. We have witnessed — and continue to witness — the folly of discredited academics in music and painting who, finding themselves unable to judge by the standards of previous generations, refuse to judge at all and — as academics always will — look favourably only on work whose styles and motives are easily recognized. Recognition, indeed, is the key word. The successful play in London's West End is as likely to meet approval because characters and situations can be "recognized" (therefore the audience is comfortable) as it is because it has any original merit. A theatre dominated by Tom Stoppard and Andrew Lloyd Webber is neither vital nor original. One feels sorry for many of these thin, parsimonious souls. The popular revival of full-blooded, highly disciplined romanticism could turn all their notions upside down.

With new aesthetic standards emerging, new battles must be fought, but in the meantime honest vulgarity, so long as it is not brutal or humourless, is always preferable to hypocrisy and caution. If we must be given stories about talking animals let them at least be sceptical, sardonic and world-weary talking animals. Better still, a book-length romance about a family of ferrets would make a welcome antidote to the sentimental, quasi-romantic drivel presently filling the "Fantasy" sections of our bookshops. ("You'll never guess what's for tea, darlings. It's Pooh-and-Pippin pie!")

But that, I suppose, would be the most unlikely fantasy of them all.

Sources

Partial bibliographies of the main writers mentioned in this book have been published in various Lin Carter anthologies. These anthologies are no longer in print, but it might be worth trying to obtain them through second-hand booksellers since they are very useful and recommended to anyone who wishes to sample the work I have described. They are not very accurate on bibliographical facts, but they are a fair guide. The books are published in paperback by Ballantine/Pan (USA/UK) and are: *Dragons, Elves, and Heroes*, 1969 (Morris, Malory etc.) and *The Young Magicians*, 1969 (Dunsany, Eddison, Cabell etc.).

Carter's *Imaginary Worlds*, 1973, is a book about epic fantasy. Although academically not too good and sometimes downright inaccurate, this book contains an extensive bibliography. It is remarkable, as are most Carter anthologies, for the self-esteem of the author, who never hesitates to mention his own work, no matter how inappropriately!

Carter's rather unfortunately named (for the UK, at least) anthologies of modern epic fantasy are the four volumes in the *Flashing Swords* series. These contain work by Carter, Anderson, Leiber, Vance, Jakes, Norton, de Camp, Katherine Kurtz and Avram Davidson.

Michael Ashley's *Who's Who in Horror and Fantasy*, 1978, is also very useful. I would recommend his anthology *Jewels of Wonder*, 1981.

For various essays on Tolkien, Lewis and Charles Williams I would recommend the collection edited by Mark Hillegas, *Shadows of the Imagination*, 1969. Another excellent collection (including Dunsany, MacDonald, Tolkien, Lewis, Le Guin, Buchan, Cabell etc. — as well as a rare and welcome appearance from the Russian, Alexander Grin) is *The Fantastic Imagination*, 1977, edited by Robert H. Boyer and Kenneth Zahorski. The same editors also produced a collection *Fantasists on Fantasy*, 1984, in which eighteen writers discuss their view of the subject. There are also, from Zahorski and Boyer, *The Fantastic Imagination II*, *The Phoenix Tree* and *Visions of Wonder*, all anthologies, and a great many academic studies of fantasy now, usually, but not always, the work of somewhat unoriginal scholars. I can also recommend *Realms of Fantasy*, 1983, an excellent introduction to most of the major writers of fantasy: Peake, Howard, Le Guin, Tolkien etc., written by Malcolm Edwards and Robert Holdstock, and the *Elsewhere* anthologies edited by Terri Windling and Mark Alan Arnold.

Readers who wish to see or buy the books mentioned here are recommended to the various dealers who specialize in fantasy or science fiction. While it is always worth checking your Yellow Pages to find out if a bookseller near you specializes in fantasy and sf (many used book shops are increasingly devoting space to these genres), I am giving a partial list of booksellers who are likely to help you find the titles you want. All the booksellers are willing to deal with mail order customers and many stock both new and second-hand titles, having a good supply of out-of-print books and usually issuing regular catalogues. There are often one or two specialist dealers in most major British and American cities, though they are sometimes a little hard to track down. For readers who are unusually determined, I would recommend *A Directory of Dealers in Science Fiction and Fantasy*.

United States
The SF Shop, 56 Eighth Avenue, New York, N.Y. 10014 (Tel. 212–741–0270)

Forbidden Planet, 821 Broadway, New York, N.Y. 10003 (Tel. 212–473–1576)

The Old Bookstore, 210 E. Cuyahoga Falls Ave., Akron, Ohio 44310

Dangerous Visions, 13603 Ventura Blvd, Sherman Oaks, California

Dark Carnival, 2812 Telegraph Avenue, Berkeley, California 94705 (Tel. 415–845–7757)

Lloyd Currey, Elizabethtown, New York, N.Y. 12932 (Tel. 518–873–6477)

United Kingdom

Forbidden Planet, 23 Denmark Street, London WC2H 8NN (Tel. 01–836–4179) (and branches)

Phantasmagoria Books, 8 Colwell Road, E. Dulwich, London SE 22

Fantast (Medway) Ltd., PO Box 23, Upwell, Wisbech, Cambs. PE14 9BU

Fantasy Centre, 157 Holloway Road, London N7 (Tel. 01–607–9433)

Australia

Galaxy Bookshop, 106 Bathurst Street, Sydney 200 (Tel. 02–267–7630)

Unfortunately it is impossible to list more than the above. Most dealers also stock specialist magazines (such as *Locus*) which advertise booksellers and publishers, specialist collectors, conventions and so on. *Locus* is available from PO Box 13305, Oakland, California 94661, USA (or can be obtained via Fantast (Medway) Ltd in the UK). The *Directory of Dealers in Science Fiction and Fantasy*, although primarily concerned with British and American booksellers, does list some international dealers. It is available from the editor, Frank M. Halpern, Haddonfield House, Haddonfield, New Jersey 08033, USA.

Most of the best Gothic romances and other 18th- and 19th century fiction mentioned in this book are available in cheap editions from publishers like Everyman, Signet and Penguin. Recently published is a new edition of *Melmoth the Wanderer*, edited and introduced by Alethea Hayter, which I have not read, but it seems to be by far the best modern edition available (Penguin, 1977). Regarded by many as the best book on the Romantic Movement in general is Mario Praz's *The Romantic Agony*, 1933, reprinted in a revised edition by Oxford University Press, 1970. I am aware that I have not made much mention of the important influences of either the German or the French Romantic movements. Praz is an excellent source for people wishing to know more about these movements. I would also recommend Alethea Hayter's books, such as *Opium and the Romantic Imagination*; Praz's *The Hero in Eclipse in Victorian Fiction*; and R. D. Spector's collection of shorter work by Walpole, Mary Shelley, Lewis, Reeve, Poe, Hawthorne and Le Fanu, *Seven Masterpieces of Gothic Horror* (which includes a very useful bibliography for someone with access to a decent library).

I would also recommend James Cawthorn's *Fantasy: The 100 Best* (due in 1988 from Xanadu Books).

Books on the French symbolists and the surrealists will also add perspective to the subject. The best general book on the Pre-Raphaelites is probably *The Pre-Raphaelites* by Timothy Hilton (Thames & Hudson) while the best general book on fantasy illustrators is probably Brigid Peppin's *Fantasy: The Golden Age of Fantastic Illustration* (Watson-Guptill, USA/Carter Nash Cameron, UK).

Readers who look for work by George Meredith, who is mentioned frequently throughout this book, will have to find most of it in second-hand bookshops. The majority of his work is no longer in print. Ironically there are more books in print about him and his novels than there are novels by him. Usually *The Ordeal of Richard Feverel*, *The Egoist* and *Diana of the Crossways* are available, while Ballantine reprinted the rather mannered and untypical *The Shaving of Shagpat* in their Adult Fantasy series. His late masterpiece which in my view is his crowning achievement, *The Amazing Marriage*, has not been available in a new edition for years. I am surprised that the feminist presses, who have reprinted *Diana*, have not thought it worth republishing this, his most powerful attack on the condition of women in Western society. It is worth seeking out.

Finally, I would recommend *The Exploits of Engelbrecht* by Maurice Richardson. These tales of the Surrealist Sporting Club have little to do with epic fantasy, but are an excellent and extremely funny antidote for anyone suffering a surfeit of dungeons, dragons, unicorns, tremendous quests and irredeemable evil. It was published by Gray Walls Press in 1950, reprinted by John Conquest in 1977, and remains elusive. Anyone prepared to undertake the quest in pursuit of it will find themselves well rewarded when they read of "The Night of the Big Witch Shoot" or "The Day We Played Mars".

Michael Moorcock,
London, December 1985
Oxford, July 1987

Index

TITLES AVAILABLE FROM
VGSF

The prices shown below were correct at the time
of going to press (March 1988)

☐ 04008 4	HEGIRA	*Greg Bear*	£2.95
☐ 04090 4	STRENGTH OF STONES	*Greg Bear*	£2.95
☐ 04009 2	ANGEL WITH THE SWORD	*C.J. Cherryh*	£2.95
☐ 04044 0	THE DREAMSTONE	*C.J. Cherryh*	£2.50
☐ 04043 2	THE TREE OF SWORDS AND JEWELS		
		C. J. Cherryh	£2.95
☐ 03988 4	THE OTHER SIDE OF THE SKY		
		Arthur C. Clarke	£2.95
☐ 04199 4	BUY JUPITER	*Isaac Asimov*	£2.95
☐ 03995 7	WITCH WORLD	*Andre Norton*	£2.50
☐ 03996 5	WEB OF THE WITCH WORLD	*Andre Norton*	£2.50
☐ 03999 X	YEAR OF THE UNICORN	*Andre Norton*	£2.50
☐ 03998 1	THREE AGAINST THE WITCH WORLD		
		Andre Norton	£2.50
☐ 03997 3	WARLOCK OF THE WITCH WORLD		
		Andre Norton	£2.50
☐ 04007 6	STAR GATE	*Andre Norton*	£2.50
☐ 04124 2	STAR MAN'S SON	*Andre Norton*	£2.50
☐ 03989 2	TO LIVE AGAIN	*Robert Silverberg*	£2.95
☐ 04038 6	UP THE LINE	*Robert Silverberg*	£2.95
☐ 04040 8	THE TIME HOPPERS	*Robert Silverberg*	£2.95
☐ 04032 7	THE FACELESS MAN	*Jack Vance*	£2.50
☐ 04053 X	THE BRAVE FREE MEN	*Jack Vance*	£2.50
☐ 04052 1	THE ASUTRA	*Jack Vance*	£2.50
☐ 04022 X	MISSION OF GRAVITY	*Hal Clement*	£2.50
☐ 04096 3	MEDUSA'S CHILDREN	*Bob Shaw*	£2.50
☐ 04090 4	WHO GOES HERE?	*Bob Shaw*	£2.95
☐ 04011 4	EARTHWIND	*Robert Holdstock*	£2.95
☐ 04023 8	IN THE VALLEY OF THE STATUES		
		Robert Holdstock	£2.95
☐ 04125 0	QUEST OF THE THREE WORLDS		
		Cordwainer Smith	£2.50

Also available: VGSF CLASSICS

☐ 03819 5	THE SIRENS OF TITAN	*Kurt Vonnegut*	£3.50
☐ 03821 7	MORE THAN HUMAN	*Theodore Sturgeon*	£3.50

Continued overleaf

☐ 03820 9	A TIME OF CHANGES	*Robert Silverberg*	£3.50
☐ 03849 7	THE CITY AND THE STARS	*Arthur C. Clarke*	£3.50
☐ 03850 0	THE DOOR INTO SUMMER	*Robert Heinlein*	£3.50
☐ 03851 9	THE REPRODUCTIVE SYSTEM	*John Sladek*	£3.50
☐ 03978 7	A FALL OF MOONDUST	*Arthur C. Clarke*	£3.50
☐ 03979 5	ROGUE MOON	*Algis Budrys*	£3.50
☐ 03981 7	MAN PLUS	*Frederik Pohl*	£3.50
☐ 03993 0	INVERTED WORLD	*Christopher Priest*	£3.50
☐ 04061 0	FLOWERS FOR ALGERNON	*Daniel Keyes*	£3.50
☐ 04122 6	JOURNEY BEYOND TOMORROW		
		Robert Sheckley	£3.50
☐ 04144 7	DANGEROUS VISIONS	*ed. by Harlan Ellison*	£6.95
☐ 04123 4	BABEL-17	*Samuel R. Delany*	£3.95
☐ 04127 7	GLADIATOR-AT-LAW		
		Frederik Pohl & C. M. Kornbluth	£3.95
☐ 04121 8	BRING THE JUBILEE	*Ward Moore*	£3.95
☐ 04134 X	BEASTS	*John Crowley*	£3.95
☐ 04195 1	RENDEZVOUS WITH RAMA	*Arthur C. Clarke*	£2.95
☐ 03994 9	THE SPACE MACHINE	*Christopher Priest*	£3.50

All these books are available at your shop or newsagent or can be ordered direct from the publisher. Just tick the titles you want and fill in the form below.

VGSF, Cash Sales Department, PO Box 11, Falmouth, Cornwall.

Please send cheque or postal order, no currency.

Please allow cost of book(s) plus the following for postage and packing:

UK customers – Allow 60p for the first book, 25p for the second book plus 15p for each additional book ordered, to a maximum charge of £1.90.

BFPO – Allow 60p for the first book, 25p for the second book plus 15p per copy for the next seven books, thereafter 9p per book.

Overseas customers including Eire – Allow £1.25 for the first book, 75p for the second book plus 28p for each additional book ordered.

NAME *(Block letters)* ....

ADDRESS ....

....

....